"Understanding the healing power of our creativity is essential to any-one creating a balanced life. This book is a great resource and an inspir-ing read on the subject." **John Weeks**, *former Executive Director, Academic Consortium for Complementary and Alternative Healthcare and The Integrator Blog* (www.theintegratorblog.com)

"There is a profound connection between inner health and creativity. We are only now waking up to the immensity of our creative potential to heal our lives and our world. This book shows us why the time and place is here and now." - **Benjo Masilungan, MD**

Creativity Unzipped: Why Your Thoughts Matter is a call to action for each one of us to claim our creative voice--in whatever form it materializes--and express it in the world. - **Maureen Murdock**, author of *The Heroine's Journey and Unreliable Truth: On Memoir and Memory*

"This book is full of wisdom, encouragement and hope. It expands the definition of creativity so everyone can feel creative and see the impor-tance of their contributions. Just what we need: a why-to book on the subject!" **Lily Yeh,** *founder, Barefoot Artists Project*

"In *Creativity Unzipped,* Phillips and Westreich take a plunge into the deep well of creativity and all its forms, including artistic and cognitive ideation and execution. Inspiration often happens without brushstroke, pen or piano key. Its impact from an economic, social, physical and emotional standpoint is frequently profound but often immeasurable. Phillips and Westreich teach us why nurturing a pro-creativity environ-ment should be a national responsibility to bequeath to future genera-tions." **Glenn Sabin, Fon Consulting Founder,** *author of 'n of 1': How One Man's Triumph Over Incurable Cancer is Changing the Medical Establishment*

"Jan and Ruth open door after door to the unique creative energy within each one of us. If you fear that you are not creative as many people do, you'll discover a different story here. Open it and see." **Seena Frost**, *founder/author, Soul Collage*

"Jan Phillips and Ruth Westreich give heart to all of us to be evolutionary creators, to become visionary leaders sharing from our lived experiences. They give us permission to take the time to create and contribute to the fabric of our culture and legacy. I love the full range of creative gestures that Phillips and Westreich embrace. It is wide enough for all of us." **Elizabeth Murray**, author o*f Living Life in Full Bloom*

"This book explores creative consciousness with laser focus. It simplifies a complex concept with profound elegance." **Shamini Jain, PhD**, *Executive Director Consciousness and Healing Institute, Assistant professor, Department of Psychiatry at UC San Diego*

"No book marries creativity and healing like this one does. A must read!" **Naj Wykoff,** *Arts and Health Alliance*

"Informed by generous heart, enlivened by true stories and grounded in research, *Creativity Unzipped* is an essential read and invaluable reference for anyone interested in enhanced personal and global health, creative well-being and ecology ... and that means EVERYONE. I love how Jan and Ruth debunk excuses, false beliefs and fears of practicing our human birthright of full creative expression ever more essential at this tipping point in global history.**Aviva Gold, MFA, ATR, LCSW**, Author of *Painting From The Source: Awakening The Artists Soul In Everyone* and *Source Art In The World*

"While there are many things I admire about this "why-to book on creativity", what I admire most is its foundational premise - the recognition that we are creation looking back upon itself, and thus creativity is our very nature. As such, creativity isn't something that needs to be developed but rather untethered, and done so through a deliberate movement towards responsibility and self-authority. This is a lovely book that can help get us there, and reminds us why it is important to create at all."
Paul J. Mills, PhD, *Professor of Family Medicine and Public Health, Professor of Psychiatry; Director, Integrative Health and Mind-Body Biomarker Laboratory: Director of Research, Deepak Chopra Center*

CREATIVITY UNZIPPED

CREATIVITY UNZIPPED

WHY YOUR THOUGHTS MATTER

Jan Phillips and Ruth Westreich

Creativity Unzipped
Why Your Thoughts Matter

First edition
ISBN-13: 9780692695517
ISBN-10: 0692695516

Published by Livingkindness Foundation
5187 Arlene Place
San Diego, CA 92117

Cover design by Ruth Westreich
Interior graphs by Ruth Westreich

Printed and bound in United States of America

www.livingkindness.org
www.janphillips.com
www.ruthwestreichtheartist.com

TABLE OF CONTENTS

INTRODUCTION

*I know artists whose medium is life itself, and who express
the inexpressible without brush, pencil, chisel or guitar. They
neither paint, nor dance. Their medium is Being. Whatever
their hand touches has increased life….They are the artists of
being alive.*
FREDERICK FRANCK

"YOU'RE LUCKY YOU'RE so creative," I heard someone say to Ruth at an exhibition of our photographs from the American Southwest.

"You're lucky, too" Ruth replied. "We're all creative, just in different ways."

"Oh not me," said the woman. "I don't have a creative bone in my body."

"Well, I never believed that about myself," said Ruth. "Maybe that's what's made all the difference."

Our beliefs shape us. Unfortunately, we inherit many of our beliefs from a society that doesn't foster self-expression or original thinking. For some reason, our cultural definition of creativity makes most people feel excluded, which is what we address in this book. While the two of us have chosen paths in life that could be characterized as "artistic," the case we are making about creativity is that it doesn't necessarily have to be associated with the arts. Creativity, the way we define it, has more to do with how we create our lives, how we use the tools of imagination and intention to shape the lives we inhabit.

If you are alive and breathing, you are in the process of creating your daily events, creating the environment you live in, creating the story of your life. All day long you make things happen, and at the end of each day, you can look back and see what you created.

We designed a survey to get at the core of the issue and sent it out to our lists of friends and followers. More than 1,200 people responded, and we learned a great deal about what stops people, what fears they have, what voices sabotage their beliefs in themselves. While a majority of respondents acknowledged that they were creative, a vast number admitted to deep hesitancy when it comes to actually expressing it.

Ruth is a painter, photographer and jeweler. She is also a social philanthropist who is working with academics, scientists and health care professionals on initiatives that raise awareness about whole-person health and resilience. Ruth created and directs the Westreich Foundation which works in nonprofit education and leadership.

As an artist, Jan is a writer, a musician, video producer and photographer. She co-created and directs the Livingkindness Foundation which has built the Livingkindness Centre for Learning in Ikuzeh, Nigeria in collaboration with the NGO Hope for the Village Child. As the writer in this collaboration, I am the one who is weaving together our thoughts and putting our ideas into words.

We are both committed creators who believe that our thoughts, words, and actions are the most important tools we have when it comes to creativity. And while we are both committed to the fine arts, producing paintings, photographs, books, music, the creativity we speak of here is the act of creating our lives. Our mission is twofold: to deconstruct myths about creativity that have silenced us for so long and to redefine the meaning of "creative" so everyone feels included.

This mission comes in response to what we see as a fundamental need. Our world needs our voices now. It needs to hear our values, our visions. If we do not contribute to the shaping of our communities and culture, then big business will do it for us. Corporations are more than happy to usurp the public commons, and when they do, it is *their* values that get disseminated. In many cases, it is profit that matters more than people.

Every institution we grew up with is in trouble now. It's not just our physical infrastructure that needs repair and tending. Our moral infrastructure is caving in all around us. It's harder and harder for the prophetic voices to be heard. The Hopi elder said, "We are the ones we've been waiting for," and yet people throw their arms up in the air, feeling powerless. This book is an antidote to that. It is medicine for the soul, fire for the imagination, a map to the buried treasures within.

The insight we need for these times resides inside us. This book will help you tap into your wisdom and imagine new ways of sharing it. Centuries ago, the Sufi mystic Rumi said, "Stop learning, start knowing." You don't need more information. You need to clarify what you know and figure out how to share it. Every experience of your life is grist for your creative mill. The knowledge to do what you need to do you already have. It's what you acquired as you survived all those tragedies and breakdowns. You've been creating your life for all these years. Now you can do it with more precision, more purpose. You already know *how* to do it. This book is to help you remember *why* to do it. This book is our Tibetan gong, our cathedral chimes, our shofar sounding a call to action. It is our hope that it opens all kinds of doors and windows to your creative self.

CHAPTER 1

BORN TO CREATE, BRED TO FEAR: WHY YOU HAVE MORE CREATIVE BLOCKS THAN BUILDING BLOCKS

Turning on the light is easy if you know where the switch is.
COLIN WILSON

WHAT IS CREATIVITY?

CREATIVITY IS AMONG the most abstract subjects humans have ever tried to study. Thousands of books, articles, and pieces are written about creativity, but there is no particular place in the human body where one can go to explore it microscopically. It is not a function of the brain alone. No one knows for certain why some people are more creative or artistic than others, what part is nature and what part is nurture, or what any of us can do to become more creative in our approach to life. As for a simple definition, neuroscientists and cognitive researchers agree that an idea or response is creative if it is: 1) novel or original; 2) useful or functional; and 3) surprising or non-obvious.

It would be impossible for any of us to navigate through a normal day without generating a few original ideas that are useful and completely surprising. That's how our brains work. We are born creators. When we meet with an obstacle, we create a solution. Even art-making in itself is a problem-solving endeavor. While some neuroscientists assert that all humans are innately creative to different degrees,[1] other research suggests that our brains are hardwired to fear creativity.[2]

According to Dartmouth College psychologist Alexander Schlegel, lead author of a paper published in the journal *NeuroImage*, creativity is

1

a concept that is often thought of as something we are either born with or will never have, but his data refutes that notion. He writes,

> Maybe there are gene variants that give individuals a proclivity toward art (e.g. make them more open to new ideas or more prone to make connections or see patterns), but that is a long way from saying they were born an artist and that those without such gene variants are doomed to being uncreative. It also propagates the strange myth of the artist as a special class of human. I hope our study will help to debunk the notion that there are "artists" and "the rest of us."[3]

Intellectually, it is a deep and mysterious subject, but each one of us knows *something* about creativity from our own personal experience. Every one of us has experienced the act of creativity. We have created relationships, environments, adventures. Just think of the things that exist in the world because you are alive and creative. You have an idea about something, you feel a desire for that thing, you begin to speak about it, make steps toward it, and soon it is part of your reality.

We're hardwired to find creative solutions to complex problems, but there's a problem with our software—our inherited beliefs and cultural conditioning. We're stymied by negative background noise that begins, for many of us, during childhood. How many times have you heard the expression, "I'm not creative. I can't draw a straight line?" The statement itself makes no sense. There is little correlation between straight lines and creativity. The contours of our lives, the look and feel of our cultures and our communities all stem from our own birthright for creativity. Everything we do or fail to do impacts this civilization, which has our signatures all over it.

To a great extent, our lives are in our own hands. There is no Geppetto pulling our strings. No outside force is causing things to happen. *We* cause things to happen. Just as a sculptor shapes materials with her hands, we shape our experiences with our thoughts and actions. When we speak of creativity in this book, we are simultaneously referring to its two aspects: the act of creating our lives and the practice of artistic endeavor. We are two women who are deeply engaged in both processes—mindful that each day is shaped by our choices.

It's not that we're unique or immune to the cultural conditioning that discourages creative expression. Both of us have experienced its full force, but somehow we've been resilient against its negative drag. As two women whose lives are lived largely in the public domain—teaching, facilitating, circling, listening—we hear repeatedly from people who feel disempowered creatively, who feel inept, self-conscious, and silenced. This book has a different message: *You already know everything you need to know to be a fully expressed, creative agent.*

You have learned enough. You do not need another how-to book. Your research is done, for the time being, and it is time now to make something of what you know, of what your experiences have taught you. As Meister Eckhart, the German mystic, reminds us, *the process of enlightenment is one of subtraction, not addition.* To become luminous, we must let go of the darkness, let go of our negative beliefs. Luminous is our natural state. We are children of the light, born from exploding stars and supernovae. As Carl Sagan said in *Cosmos,* "The nitrogen in our DNA, the calcium in our teeth, the iron in our blood, the carbon in our apple pies were made in the interiors of collapsing stars. We are made of starstuff."[4] Our actual material value is about three dollars' worth of chemicals, but when you add the worth of our imaginations, our brains and creativity, our value expands exponentially. Our true worth is buried within us, and creativity is the act of mining and harvesting it.

So the journey is not out into the fray, but inward toward the wisdom within. The work, first, is to look back and see how you were silenced or shamed about your own generative powers, to see that it's not your fault. It is not personal. It happens to everyone. It's a social phenomenon.

You don't even need to go into the why of this phenomenon to understand its relationship to economics, though it may help to realize that our free-market system only works if people are made to feel they are not okay unless they buy the products that are being marketed to them. Everyone has to go through an awakening on the journey into maturity and that process need not end in anger or blame. If you are simply aware of the messages you've received all your life and understand why you're hesitant about your own originality or creativity, then you are ready to rise above the noise.

Most messages we receive negate our birthright, our inherent power to create. The average person sees or hears about 250 advertisements per day.[5] Every message is designed to make us look outside for fulfillment instead of inside for meaning and joy. We are a consumer-driven society, trying to keep up with the Joneses. If you're fifty years old, you've been exposed to more than four-and-a-half million messages—programming—that say you're not okay just as you are—that you need this product, this car, this insurance, this perfume, this pill. Research shows that exposure to non-stop negativity impairs brain function.[6] So the more we absorb and assimilate those messages, the less likely we are to be creatively productive.

While the scientific community divides creativity up into everyday creativity (solving problems) and higher levels of creativity (engaging in artistic endeavors), we synthesize the two into one category that refers to the innate capacity of all humans to think originally and act creatively. We are born to create, fully equipped and responsible for co-creating our lives, our local cultures, and, ultimately, our global civilization.

In many ways, the word "creativity" has been in a cultural pigeonhole; its association with the fine arts has led people to believe they are not creative if they are not involved in painting, music, dance, poetry, or the visual arts. This categorization has undermined the brilliance of a large portion of the population. It has led to a society of individuals who feel life is happening *to* them, rather than *through* them. As they abdicate the power of their imagination and creativity, the fire in the belly turns to smoke, and people end up suffocating their own passions and leading diminished lives.

The myth that only a select few are creative has contributed to a world of disparities. We all know the trouble we're in. We all feel the daily news dragging down our spirits. And it's hard to imagine solving problems if we can't acknowledge our creative potential, if we hold onto the notion that "he's got the whole world in his hands." When a politician says it is blasphemous to worry about climate change because it doesn't acknowledge God's will in the matter, one can't help but wonder if that's an attempt to exonerate humanity from responsibility.

That's the power of outmoded cultural myths. They don't keep up with our evolutionary pace. We can forgive our ancestors for not knowing any better, but our grandchildren won't forgive us for turning our backs on problems that need our creativity right now. We have a lot of power. Our choices and actions make all the difference. It is irresponsible today for anyone to think he or she is not creative. We impact and influence our culture with our stories, our consumer habits, our civic actions, our votes, our creations, and our media consumption. The world we live in is directly correlated with what we want to see and how we let our desires and demands be known.

Every day, technology and science open up more arenas where human intelligence has an influence. As human citizens, we are at choice points and crossroads all the time. Information is coming our way at warp speed, and we get to make something of it. We absorb it and metabolize it, according to our creative consciousness. Just as cells metabolize food for the well-being of the entire body, so are we designed to transform information for the well-being of the global family. That is what our creativity is all about.

As photosynthesis enabled the planet to evolve biologically, we too are experiencing a phenomenon enabling us to evolve consciously. We ourselves are agents of a new transformation, engaged in a process of "infosynthesis" whereby we convert intelligence into inspiration through the creative power of our imagination. There is a purposefulness to each *natural* act—when the trees transform carbon dioxide into oxygen, it sustains humanity and allows us to breathe. When one person transforms his or her ideas or experiences into stories, songs, theater, etc., it sustains the rest of us on a soul level. It helps us live more fully, to feel connected. Imagine a world with no Beethoven, no Michelangelo, no Galileo, no Marie Curie, no Elizabeth Cady Stanton, no Rosa Parks. We could not have become who we are without the benefit of each other's creativity.

BORN TO CREATE

This book is a result of Ruth and me asking each other how can we help create a culture that won't disappoint future generations. We are not willing to respond silently to the phrase, "How can I do anything? I'm not creative. I can't draw a straight line." For many reasons, this is unacceptable, irresponsible. Yes, we were all programmed for silence, but we can find our voices and speak from our hearts about what matters. It's courageous to create because we live in a culture established by people who didn't know what we know about creativity.

This culture is not a perfect receptacle for many of our creations, but we help to make it so as we continue to create. The more we put our words and our works into the public domain, the more the public domain, the culture itself, evolves forward. It's the brave and committed ones who step up—not those who were properly programmed, but those who are passionately moved.

You do not need to be raised in a creative environment in order to become a creative and creating person. In my childhood home, there were few books or bookshelves. The only magazines that arrived regularly were *Popular Science* and *Popular Mechanics* for my father. As for art, there was one large print of a sunset over the couch and one painting of poppies in a vase, not original. A set of *Encyclopedia Britannica* from the 1940s lined a small shelf.

I experienced one art class in eight years of education at St. Anthony of Padua School. It was in fifth grade. Mrs. Kearns opened up a box of 5x7 cards. They were botanical paintings of birds and flowers, and she instructed us to pass them on from one to another down the rows. There were forty-eight students in the classroom—six rows and eight desks per row—and the exercise had to be done in silence. Get a card. Look at it. Appreciate it, then pass it on. That was the day I discovered I hated art.

As for creativity, my ideas on that were shaped as much by what wasn't said as what was. In Catholic school, they taught us *what* to think, not *how* to think. If a subject wasn't mentioned, one could assume it wasn't important. Creativity never came up.

For Ruth, creativity surfaced organically as a response to early childhood trauma. From her toddler years, she witnessed her alcoholic father abuse her mother until he was killed in a car accident. From elementary school on, she was caretaker for her mother, who was born with a hole in her heart. As an only child, she had no one to help her process her reality, so she took to drawing. It was calming for her, and as she turned to it more and more frequently, her skills improved greatly.

What kept her motivated to be creative in her thinking, actions, and being was that failing at anything for her was not an option. She drew as a way to create a safe space to entertain herself and keep busy. There was not a lot of nurturing in her house and when there was, it was Ruth nurturing her mother, as she describes here.

One school of thought says you pick your parents. Another school of thought says it is the luck of the draw wherever you land. Whichever school of thought you are more drawn to doesn't matter. What does matter is that no matter what your early childhood circumstances, you don't let them define you as a person. You let them inform who you are in the world and what you do with your life in the service of others.

I have mentored many young women with childhoods similar to mine, helping them cope with home lives that are untenable, helping them find positive ways to cope until they were able to be on their own. And they have all gone on to lead productive lives.

Developing my creativity on my own was like being thrown into a swimming pool to learn to swim. I didn't have a guide or mentor to help me navigate the rough waters. I remember thinking that there were people just out of my reach who could help me find some answers, but I had no way to find them. I had to sink or swim, which was definitely the hard way to learn, but it worked. Nothing was too difficult to tackle, whether it be learning to fix a broken toilet, sewing my clothes, or painting our apartment. By the time I was ten, I was pretty self-sufficient. In every way possible, I tried to create 'a normal happy home' because failing was not an option.

In the early stages of writing this book, we sent a creativity survey out to our mailing lists and were initially surprised to learn how high the percentage was of people who considered themselves creative. Out of 1,206 responses, 1,121 (92.9 percent) defined themselves as creative.[7] Because our audience is mostly women dedicated to self-realization and the betterment of the planet, this shouldn't have been surprising. Since we believe that being creative *brings about* inspiration as much as the other way around, we imagine that a more inspiring culture will be created by individuals who are engaged in creative work and original thinking.

In a global study conducted by Adobe in 2012, five thousand adults from the United States, the United Kingdom, Germany, France, and Japan were interviewed about their creativity. Their results were substantially different than ours, and they went into areas we didn't explore. In Adobe's study, 39 percent described themselves as creative, but only 25 percent of the people interviewed believed they were living up to their creative potential.[8]

More than half of the respondents felt the educational system stifles creativity. They reported increasing pressure to be productive rather than creative at work. In the United States and the United Kingdom, 80 percent of people felt that way, while the number rose as high as 85 percent in France. Americans indicated that they believed the United States is the most creative of all the countries, but they expressed the strongest concern that they were not being true to their creative potential, even though 76 percent of them believed that being creative is valuable to society.[9]

So why these incongruences? When so many consider creativity to be a good thing, why are so few actually creating? We posed a question to see if people were defining *creative* and *artistic* in the same way. As it turns out, a huge majority of respondents said no.

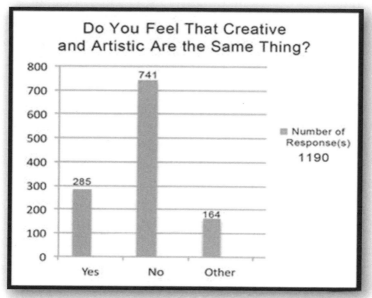

Phillips/Westreich Creativity Survey, 2014. (PW002)

Here are a few of the responses we received, in the words of respondents themselves.

"Creative means generative. Artistic is more a feel or style."
"Being artistic requires specific training. Creativity requires a way of thinking."
"Creativity doesn't always include an artistic output."
"Creative is thinking processes. Artistic is conscious commitment."

From our perspective, creativity has a lot to do with finding one's voice and expressing it into the world. People make up stories all day long about what happened in the office, at the gas station, while walking the dog, or while waiting in the doctor's office. We are story machines. Notice how quickly you want to make up a story and tell it to someone every time things don't go the way you want. It comes naturally, and yet people don't consider this a creative act. Why is that? We create a beginning, a middle, an end, a hero (ourselves, usually), a villain, a conflict, and a resolution. Our propensity for story is ever with us. We know the joy of creating and sharing narratives that are original, useful, and surprising to ourselves and to others. We begin to see, in a more subtle way, how our speaking creates an ambiance, how our stories cause others to re-imagine their own stories. It doesn't matter if our stories are all about us. Those who listen imagine themselves as the heroes, wondering what *they* might do given the same circumstances.

In a way, the stories we tell help us to walk a mile in each others' shoes, to have empathy for the person we stand shoulder-to-shoulder with—and in turn, they for us. No matter what our motivations, relating stories to one another creates relationships among narrators and listeners. Those relationships may last three minutes (at the grocery store, perhaps), but the relationships would not have existed without the story. And in some cases, an intimacy is formed.

While there may be some fear associated with this idea of intimacy, it's important to consider how the fear compares to the isolation you may feel when you fail to show up, fail to self-express. Psychoanalyst Rollo May, author of *The Courage to Create*, writes, "If you do not express your own original ideas, if you do not listen to your own being, you will have betrayed yourself."[10] This is eerily close to the words of Thomas, in the Gnostic Gospel: "If you bring forth what is within you, what you bring forth will save you. If you do not bring forth what is within you, what you do not bring forth will destroy you."[11]

Bringing forth what is within you may pale in comparison to the idea of calling yourself a creator. Or the reverse may be true. It all depends on what you were told about creativity or about your own value. Beliefs we inherit at an early age are hard to release, especially when we are vulnerable and trusting of adults who, intentionally or not, ingrain those beliefs in us. But if you consider all the ideas you were exposed to that you eventually abandoned, it may be easier than you think to dismantle this one and step into your role as a conscious creator.

You may find some inspiration in the words of Henry Miller, a novelist, travel writer, and watercolorist.

> Every day we slaughter our finest impulses. That is why we get a headache when we read those lines written by the hand of a master and recognize them as our own, as the tender shoots which we stifled because we lacked the faith to believe in our own powers, our own criterion of truth and beauty. Every man, when he gets quiet, when he becomes desperately honest with himself, is capable of uttering profound truths.[12]

CREATIVITY AND THE BRAIN

Whether one approaches creativity from a linear, rational perspective or jumps in spontaneously for a hands-on experience, in the end, both sides of our brain are called into action. Recent neurological studies have disproved the theory that creativity comes from the right brain and rationality from the left.[13] The creative process actually involves both hemispheres of the brain and combines two types of thinking: divergent and convergent. Usually a problem-solving process begins with the generation of a number of unique associations, and an expansion of the horizon. This is called divergent thinking, and it often occurs in a free-flowing manner, where many creative ideas are generated spontaneously. Once a number of ideas emerge as possibilities to work with, the process of convergent thinking begins, where factual assessment comes into play, and those ideas are evaluated. Finally one or two are selected for elaboration. This image illustrates how divergent thinking and convergent thinking work in tandem. Ideas + Facts = Answer.

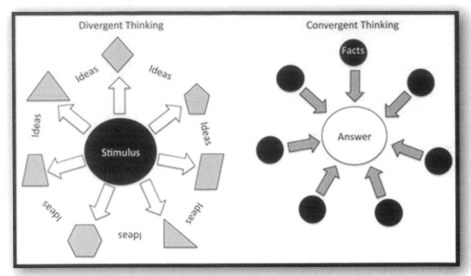

Divergent and Convergent Thinking in Tandem.
Illustration by Ruth Westreich.[14]

Think of editing your photos to make a book. Out of a hundred or two hundred images, you narrow them down to your favorite forty or fifty. Then you look again more closely and select the final twenty. It may seem simple, but the process is quite complex because the whole brain kicks into gear as arbiter of an outcome that is both beautiful and authentic.

Psychological research indicates that, even though creativity is often associated with sudden bursts of originality, creative solutions are typically the result of an enduring and long process. Amanda Gardner, writer for Health.com, documents the value that power naps bring to the creative process.[15] In our experience, *both attentiveness and rest* are integral parts of creation. We experience the gift of an idea from what *seems* an outside force, what some think of as the Muse or Spirit. This comes like a seed that needs to be planted, fertilized, and cultivated in bringing it to life. The original idea might be a song title, a line for a poem, an idea for a book. It comes unbidden and quite by surprise, sometimes in the middle of a dream, which is why we keep our journals, sketch pads, and other recording devices close to our beds.

While the brain forms millions of new associations every nanosecond of our lives, it still feels like those great ideas come from somewhere outside us, which is why some people use the word "channeling" to describe the process for them. In his book *Imagine,* Jonah Lehrer writes, "People assumed their best ideas came from somewhere else. The imagination was outsourced."[16] William James localizes the action, referring to the process as a "seething cauldron of ideas, where everything is fizzling and bobbing about in a state of bewildering activity."[17] It's different for all, and if one had to generalize, one might say it's inside *and* outside, and call it a day.

The poet Kabir says it like this.

> Take a pitcher full of water and set it down on the water
> —now it has water inside and water outside.
> We mustn't give it a name,
> lest silly people start talking again
> about the body and the soul.[18]

What we can concede is that there are certain unknowns about the creative process. Because we are all creators, we all experience the phenomenon through our own sensory apparatus. It feels different to each one of us, and there is no right or wrong way to be creative. When I told my record producer that I was going to stop recording because my voice was getting weaker and it didn't sound beautiful anymore, he said, "Do you think that ever stopped Bob Dylan or Leonard Cohen? It's not about beauty. It's about expressing what's unique to you. It's the *realness* that makes it good."

As we proceed in the act of creation, the litmus test is always about authenticity. Is this *your* voice, *your* soul, *your* story coming through this piece? The idea or seed you're cultivating has surfaced for a purpose and awaits the originality only you can bring to it. In *Milieus of Creativity,* Joachin Funke writes about this process, suggesting an inherent order to things. He lists the steps in the following order:

1. Preparation
2. Incubation
3. Insight
4. Evaluation
5. Elaboration[19]

This helps us see how divergent and convergent thinking processes come into play. Here's how the steps come to play in our own creative processes.

PHASE 1: PREPARATION

Before most creative acts, there is the preparation. The imagination visualizes something, perceives its value, and anticipates its birth and life. Endless hours are spent in contemplating, fleshing it out, imagining its parts, envisioning its delivery and impact. If it is a performance, months and years are often dedicated to practice. Malcolm Gladwell writes about the 10,000-hour rule in his book *Outliers*, asserting that one must practice approximately 10,000 hours in order to achieve mastery in a creative endeavor. Martha Graham, speaking about the great Russian ballet dancer said, 'Nijinsky took thousands of leaps before that memorable one."[20] The team that won Olympic Gold in Sochi's Figure Skating competition had been practicing together for seventeen years.

Preparing ourselves is a matter of consciousness. Placing ourselves in a state of mindfulness is a form of preparation. Every morning, I get my coffee, light my candle, and sit in silence for an hour. Perfect solitude. No phone, no e-mail, no books, no papers. When I started this practice twenty-five years ago, I committed to twenty minutes a day. I was so busy I couldn't imagine fitting in more time. But I discovered those twenty minutes were the best minutes of my day, so I kept extending my quiet time. It is my one hour when I am at peace, when all heaven breaks loose, when ideas fall like raindrops in a summer storm.

I imagine myself connected to Mind-at-Large—the Creative Force— all my channels open for reception. Thoughts arrive, and I attempt to stay focused. When my mind wanders, I start again, pay attention to my breaths, stay present and open-minded. I collect the seeds in my journal, if any come. This is my preparation for the daily creation of my life.

When Ruth prepares herself for the day, she walks silently in nature, a vessel for ideas, solutions, and direction. In the silence and with an open heart and mind, she trusts that what comes in through her is the collective consciousness imparting its wisdom.

While our practices vary, the presence we tune into remains the same, as do our intentions: we open ourselves, we quiet ourselves, we listen and work with what comes.

PHASE 2: INCUBATION

Contrary to public opinion, it's a good idea to stop and take a rest in the middle of a creative challenge. It gives the brain a chance to come at a solution from other angles. During a rest, intuitive information processing still occurs, though it remains below the level of consciousness. Scientists are trying to work out why the brain does so much when it seems to be doing nothing at all. Research on naps, meditation, and nature walks reveals that mental breaks increase productivity, replenish attention, and nurture creativity.

Neuroscientist Nancy Andreasen's most recent study delves intensively into the brains of some of today's most famous scientists and artists, including Pulitzer Prize winners and six Nobel laureates, to better understand what common traits creative geniuses share and how their brains work differently from those of others. In her talk at the Aspen Ideas Festival, Andreasen explains what she's discovered about the neural basis of creativity, which is thought to occur mainly during a state called REST (random episodic silent thought).

"This state that we call REST is a state in which the mind is working very actively, at least partially at an unconscious level, and it is a resource for creativity, for dreams, and for religious experiences," she says. "During REST, association cortices are freely communicating back and forth, without being subject to reality principles." Andreasen's hypothesis is that creative people "have an especially rich repertoire of associations [in their brain activity during REST] ... and an enhanced ability to see connections that others can't."[21]

Forbes magazine published an article in which one hundred business owners describe the *aha* moments that led to their ideas for starting their businesses. Not surprisingly, an overwhelming number of ideas surfaced when the founders were at rest or engaged in other enjoyable activities. The best ideas frequently arrive when we are *not* actively seeking them.[22]

Essayist Tim Kreider wrote in the *New York Times*,

> Idleness is not just a vacation, an indulgence or a vice; it is as indispensable to the brain as vitamin D is to the body, and deprived of it we suffer a mental affliction as disfiguring as rickets. The space and quiet that idleness provides is a necessary condition for standing back from life and seeing it whole, for making unexpected connections and waiting for the wild summer lightning strikes of inspiration—it is, paradoxically, necessary to getting any work done.[23]

Study after study has produced evidence indicating that productivity may be enhanced by giving the mind room to wander.

PHASE 3: INSIGHT

These *aha!* experiences happen when a new association of ideas passes through the threshold of consciousness, producing a flash of insight. Such a moment can happen in the midst of a shower, during a walk through nature, in a moment of rest, or even in the middle of the night. You have felt the creative impulse, made preparations to respond to it, given thought to how it will unfold and imagined bringing the new into being. Your brain has done its work and when your emotions kick in, a coupling occurs that moves your creativity into another dimension.

Studies on insight list four main characteristics of the *aha!* experience, as follows:

1. Suddenness (the experience is surprising and immediate)
2. Ease (the solution is processed without difficulty)
3. Positive effect (insights are gratifying)
4. The feeling of being right [24]

Insight occurs when there is a break in mental fixation, allowing the solution to appear as if magically.

PHASE 4: EVALUATION

This is where we examine our creative ideas for their usefulness, joyfulness, and marketability to determine which ones to pursue. Working artists take this seriously; they must think through the whole process from concept to market if they wish to make a living as creative people. Creating, as a hobby, is entirely different from creating for a living, though both are integral in their own right. If you are painting for the love of it, your evaluation process will include technical execution, the aesthetics of the piece, its color and composition, etc. If you are painting as a career, the process of evaluation is much more extensive. In addition to the process you use for creating as a hobby, when you create professionally, you also look at the market; you create a platform; you develop a network; you reach out to galleries; and you become a champion for your art.

PHASE 5: ELABORATION

A great deal happens between the original seed being planted and the actual creation coming to life. Fear sets in; confidence wanes; feedback from others impedes momentum; some lose heart, or faith, or steam. This much is true: If we do not believe in our projects, they will never see the light of day, for nothing will make its way into reality if we don't imagine it first. Our intention, our will, our commitment all provide the jet fuel for our ideas and creations. They are required ingredients to the whole creative process. That is why Ernest Holmes said, "We need a backbone instead of a wishbone."[25]

We cannot allow ourselves to cave in. We are collaborators in the ongoing creation of the universe; the only limitations we have are those we place on ourselves. Jesuit paleontologist Pierre Teilhard de Chardin wrote in *The Phenomenon of Man,* "Man only progresses by slowly elaborating from age to age the essence and the totality of a universe deposited within him."[26]

We are engaged in the profound, collective activity of the evolution of humanity. What Teilhard de Chardin calls *elaborating on the essence deposited within us,* we call creativity. We are elaborating on the details of our lives, expanding them, expounding on them. We suffer tragedies, learn to master our ordeals, and eventually turn them into books, poems, movies—things larger than ourselves. When life brings us to our knees, we breathe deep, stay centered, search for jewels amidst the dark, and when it's over, we we have something to work with.

On one level, we are creation machines, turning out stories faster than we can record them as we externalize our experiences to share with others. On another level, we are building new pathways within our brains, rewiring our neural networks, and creating new channel capacities for the reception of higher levels of intelligence. The more intention we bring to the table, the greater the levels of input and output. The more conscious we are of collaborating with Creation Itself, the greater the connection we feel to the cosmos.

Our consciousness is the foundation of what we create. Spiritual practice, mindfulness, solitude, and study elevate our inner circuitry, amplifying the potential for creativity. When we create, we are like alchemists transforming information into inspiration through the genius of our imagination.

The universe itself is broadcasting ideas for its well-being, and those ideas are making their way into the minds best prepared to receive them. As those minds engage in the creative process, works come into existence that alter the public consciousness because of their beauty, poignancy, and truthfulness. Consider the work of Dorothea Lange. During the Great Depression, she left her portrait business in San Francisco to document the displacement of the Dust Bowl farmers. When an exhibition of her images was displayed in a New York City gallery, a man who saw them was deeply moved. He was so touched by their intimacy, so drawn into the plight of the migrant workers, he felt akin to them. He wanted to help.

"But what can I do?" he thought. "I'm just a writer." But it was John Steinbeck. So he did what he could—he wrote—and created one of the seminal American novels of the twentieth century, *The Grapes of Wrath*.[27] As another man, film director John Ford, read the words of John Steinbeck, he, too, felt moved to action. Soon Americans filled theaters to see Ford's adaptation of *The Grapes of Wrath* and felt their commonness with these farmers and migrant workers. In 1989, this film was one of the first twenty-five films to be selected for preservation in the United States National Film Registry by the Library of Congress as being "culturally, historically, or aesthetically significant."[28]

Dorothea Lange could never have known the reach of her work. All she knew was that she had a tool for getting the word out, and day by day, she, being a survivor of polio herself, limped through the camps of the most destitute and shared their world in the best way she could. That changed everything.

That's what makes us creators in our culture. We share our thoughts, our stories, our images with whomever we can and trust in their power to add beauty and light to the world. We don't question how we can change the world we live in. We simply ask, "What do I love? What do I know? What do I care about?" And to the best of our abilities, we offer those answers in the most beautiful way we can.

CHAPTER 2

─────── ⌒ ───────

THE GOLD RUSH: WHY YOUR CREATIVITY HAS VALUE FOR YOU AND OTHERS

Your own self-realization is the greatest service you can render the world.

RAMANA MAHARSHI

THE FOUNDATIONS OF OUR CREATIVITY

WHEN I ASKED Ruth if she considered her creative work valuable, she shook her head no.

"What about all the times you come to your jewelry bench when you're stressed? You spend a couple hours making necklaces and brace-lets and the next thing you know, your stress is gone."

"Well, if you put it *that* way," she said, "yes, it has value."

"And do you think it has value for others?"

"Uhhh...no," she said quickly.

"I'm talking about your *creativity*, how you're creative in the world," I say. "Like how you just organized that day at your house where 40 people came together to help the Alzheimers Association come up with a template for caring for the caregiver. You cherry-picked that group. You got artists, scientists, academics, healers, and caregivers to brainstorm together. You don't call that *creative?* You don't think that has *value?*"

"OK, OK, I get it. I know it's true, but it doesn't come naturally to think of it that way. I don't automatically think that I'm creating value. I'm just living my life," she said.

20

And I reminded her that's why we're writing this book. Because it's not a default thought. We don't wake up in the morning asking ourselves what value we're going to add to anyone's day. We don't think of ourselves as creating events that alter the very communities we live in. For fifteen years I have watched Ruth Westreich stand up and stand out as one of San Diego's premier philanthropists.

She doesn't support the opera or ballet. She doesn't build buildings so she can put her name on them. She creates circles of diversity. She hosts events that are famous for their creative combustion. She gets herself on national boards so the artists will have a voice, so the group will have diversity, so her gifts as a strategic thinker can forward the mission. She will never call herself an activist and yet everything she touches changes. She causes consciousness to rise, risks to be taken, commitments to be made that never would have happened without her presence.

Yes, her paintings are exquisite, her mixed-media is original, her jewelry is breathtaking, but it's how she shows up as a creative force for good that's noteworthy. And that same potential is available to each of us. As a working artist, I do not have the means to be philanthropic in the traditional sense. But I am philanthropic with time. I dedicate days and weeks to organizing events that bring circles of people together so that we can find our tribe, in a sense, see who cares about what we care about, work with us on projects that are needed in our communities.

Because I have dedicated my time, asked people for money, created a non-profit organization called Livingkindness Foundation, there is now a learning center in a Nigerian village that will ensure the education of children in five villages. There are twenty computer stations in the center so the adult villagers are using the computers in the off hours to update themselves on new marketing methods and strategies for more successful farming. Everything is solar-powered and the center has an apartment on each end so there are always two trained teachers on site.

Dedication to a cause like this may not seem like creative work because our ideas about creativity are badly misshapen.. We inherited the notion that *creative* has something to do with art. And it certainly does, but not exclusively. Cultural creatives are people who see a need in their communities and address it. They are using their ideas, their visions, their originality to create solutions.

Among my closest friends, one couple—both of whom are sculptors—has been tutoring the children of a Mexican family next door for fifteen years. Today, the oldest girl attends the San Francisco Art Institute, the oldest boy is in law school, and the two younger children are excelling in their studies. Another friend has been meeting people in our local library for years, teaching them to read and write English. Another has started a Threshold Choir that sings songs of comfort and peace at the bedside of dying individuals.

Kate Munger, founder of the Threshold Choir movement tells how she came to start the first choir:

The seed for the Threshold Choir was planted in June of 1990 when I sang for my friend Larry as he lay in a coma, dying of HIV/AIDS. I did housework all morning and was terrified when the time came to sit by his bedside. I did what I always did when I was afraid; I sang the song that gave me courage. I sang it for 2 ½ hours. The contrast between the morning and the afternoon was profound. I felt as if I had given generously of my essence to my dear friend while I sang to him. I also found that I felt deeply comforted myself, which in turn was comforting to him...

A few years passed, and in August 1997, while driving home from Montana, I committed myself to sing for any animals I encountered that had been killed on the road. It felt good, and I continued long after that trip was over. It is still my practice. I stop whatever I am doing (except driving), turn off the radio, and sing a small song I wrote that begins "May your spirit rise safely..." These two moments, combined with my love of singing with wonderful women and being of service, were the inspiration for the Threshold Choir.[1]

Since its beginning in 2011, the Threshold Choir has grown to over 100 chapters worldwide. It is an act of compassion and generosity that these women volunteer their time to sing to people who are facing death, grief or suffering. New songs are being written and shared constantly by people who don't necessarily think of themselves as creative. The underlying motive is human kindness.

A couple years ago, early on a Saturday morning, I got an email from my friend Nadean who was starting up a Threshold Choir. Before she had a group officially organized with songbooks, she got a call to sing at the deathbed of a woman in Del Mar. Nadean put the word out to all her friends who sang and I was among them. The message gave an address and asked that we be there within two hours. I had no idea what we would sing, or even what it would feel like to sing to someone who was dying, but I decided to go.

At the last minute, I grabbed a copy of my CD *Singing for the Soul* and put a boom box in the back seat of my car. Six of us arrived to sing. The woman was in a hospital bed in the living room, facing a large window that looked out on the Pacific Ocean. She was unconscious. Three or four family members were there and they welcomed us with deep gratitude. None of us had ever done this before, but we started the CD and sang along with each song. The most amazing thing happenened. From the beginning to the end, it seemed that each song was written for this occasion. We all knew the lyrics, as we'd been singing together for over a decade, but we'd never sung them in a context of death. One after the other, the songs spoke of our oneness with the Earth, rivers returning to the Sea, the power and beauty of circles of women, the promise that we will not be left comfortless, ending with the jubilant *I'll Fly Away*.

Each of us stood around the bed, holding positions at the woman's head, feet and sides. We laid our hands on her as we sang. Tears often fell down our cheeks, not so much out of sorrow, but for the sheer beauty and poignancy of the moment. Family members sat nearby, coming and going as need be. At the end, the dying woman's sister came up to thank each of us personally. When she came to me, I said "It's as if we were practicing for this moment for the last ten years."

None of us in that group are professional musicians. Few of us read music. Some can barely carry a tune. But we showed up, not because we have confidence in our creativity, but because we know the power of presence, the healing potential of music, the magic of any group doing something together for the benefit of someone else. These are creative acts of mercy, original gestures of compassion. This is six individuals creating their lives consciously, offering themselves generously, entering into the unknown with trust that good will come of it if we give from our hearts, sing from our souls.

There were a dozen reasons why I could have said no to the invitation to show up, but the creative act was to go, to give of myself—not knowing how at the outset. We make choices all day long that create the substance and essence of our lives on earth. The creation of our lives ushers forth from the thoughts and intentions we carry in our consciousness. If our intention is to be of use, to be an agent of change, to contribute to the making of a more peaceful world, then we will act in accordance with that. Sometimes it involves the arts, and sometimes not.

Yesterday I saw a friend I hadn't seen in twenty years. She gave me a necklace made by her brother who started FromWartoPeace.com, a company that makes jewelry and art from Peace Bronze, an alloy made from disarmed and recycled nuclear weapon systems. That is clearly an example of using the arts in the process of creating culture. But cultural creatives are expressing themselves everywhere, and most often the arts are not even involved.

At the doctors office today, I read in *USA Today* about a couple in Nashville, Tennessee who are about to get married. Instead of registering at an upscale store, they set up an online fund with the Community Foundation of Middle Tennessee and are asking wedding guests to donate money to address hunger problems in their city.[2] *That* is creative!

In another section of the same paper, an article written by the founder of EMILY's List describes the impact that organization has had since its beginning.[3] In 1982, Ellen Malcolm was dismayed that not one woman in the Democratic Party had been elected to the Senate in her own right. Part of the problem was money. After hosting a breakfast for a small gathering of activists working to get women elected to public office, Malcolm and others formed an organization to raise early money that could be leveraged into real credibility to generate additional funds later. It was called EMILY's list, for "early money is like yeast."

In 1986, the group raised $100,000 for a female candidate and Rep. Barbara Mikulski was elected to the Senate. Today she is the longest serving woman in the history of the U.S. Congress. What began in the imagination of one woman was powerful enough to attract 25 women who formed the organization. Since then EMILY'S List has grown to 3 million members. Overall, they have helped elect more than 10 women to the House, 19 to the Senate, 11 governors, and hundreds to state and locals offices. Ellen Malcolm's creativity has little to do with art-making and it has changed the face of American politics.

One hour with a daily newspaper yields numerous examples of individuals and groups who are shaping the culture day and night with their creativity. And it's possible to get good news delivered to your email box if you are tired of the old "if it bleeds, it leads" approach to news gathering. I stay hopeful by subscribing to The Optimist Daily, Utne Uplifter and Yes! Magazine.

Reading accounts of people taking action, speaking out, creating news is the best way to remind ourselves that every day we have the chance to create or re-create our lives. Every day you make choices consistent with your heart's desire. You decide where you want to live and get yourself there. If it involves a move, you do the math, take one challenge at a time, and activate the plan. If you're unhappy with your work situation, you write down what you'd *like* it to be like and set out to create something consistent with that.

The important thing to recognize is that you are not a victim of the fates. You are a creative collaborator of your own life. Circumstances and situations come our way that seem out of our control, but those are simply the contexts in which we create. We may be caring for an older parent, or a bi-polar child, or dealing with an alcoholic or disabled spouse, but these are not the determining factors of our lives. They do not seal our fates. They call for an extraordinary display of imagination, an ability to be compassionate and decisive in our commitment to build a quality life for ourselves, which is our number one job. It is not selfish, although many of us have been conditioned by our cultures or religions or families to think this way.

If you have a voice inside you that admonishes you for selfish behavior, it's most likely an inherited voice and it's time to silence it. It serves no one. It is not virtuous to abandon your own needs. Two great masters have offered some wise advice in the matter. Tony De Mello, a Jesuit psychologist and retreat director often addressed this subject. "Do what you want. That's not selfish. Selfish is expecting *other* people to do what you want."

And one of India's greatest sages, Ramana Maharshi, counseled people with these words: "Your own self-realization is the greatest service you can render the world." To be self-realized means that you live a fulfilled life that is soul-sustaining for you. And from *that* place of joy and light, you offer yourself to others. You do not sacrifice your well-being in the service of selfless behavior. You do not strive for selflessness, for then what would you have to offer anyone?

If there is any striving, let it be for the awareness that your life is the one life you are here to shape. Others in our midst will be well-served by us when we meet the needs of our hearts, when we give ourselves ample time for solitude and creativity and rest. Short of this, what do we offer but our tired, frustrated, unexpressed selves? That is no gift to anyone.

I am sitting here writing this book because that's the thing I most want to be doing today. Ruth is delivering art supplies to our local high school for homeless teens because that is what she wants to be doing today. Tonight she will be hosting a dinner for academics, scientists and researchers to explore the issues of palliative care and dying with dignity and what we as a people can do about them. She created this day. She thought it up and put it in her calendar weeks ago. She wanted to do it, she saw it unfolding in her imagination, she felt the joy of it, and today she is living it. That's how it works.

To think or say that you're not creative is blasphemous. It's immature. Irresponsible. We are the creators of these times, and every word we say, every action we take is a creative act. Most of us inherited a mythology that says some Cosmic Creator determines our fate, is responsible for our lives. We also believed in Santa Claus and the Easter Bunny, but let them go when the time was ripe.

To meet the challenges of these times, there is an invitation for each of us to evolve ourselves forward, to grow our consciousness and expand our horizons. As the Buddhist priest and scholar Yasuhiko Kimura said, "The more evolved we are, the more of the universe is in our view." The more conscious we are, the more we think in terms of *we*, not *me*. The more evolved, the more we see ourselves as nature beholding nature, nature caring for nature. As we raise our levels of intelligence and intuition, we no longer feel separate and disconnected, for we feel deeply, instinctively, our oneness with life itself, similar to what Rumi spoke of in this segment of his poem *The Dream That Must Be Interpreted:*

> We began
> as a mineral. We emerged into plant life
> and into animal state, and then into being human,
> and always we have forgotten our former states,
> except in early spring when we slightly recall
> being green again.[4]

Once we identify as a creative force, become aware that our words and thoughts are the tools we must master, then we begin to take notice of our inner workings. We become aware of the sentences we speak, the thoughts we entertain. We see that we have choices in choosing our attitudes, in speaking our minds. We understand the power we have in our hands, the power to tell a story that hurts or heals. The power to add value wherever we go, or the power to decline.

CREATIVITY GETS PERSONAL

Think of the world our Millennials are inheriting. Think of the vast variety of social and environmental issues that are problematic. Because of who you are, one of these will be close to your heart. What surfaces when you think of it? Imagine that you have a magic wand, and can fix one of the challenges we face in the world. What would you fix?

Would it have to do with drugs or teen suicides or prisons? Would it be an environmental thing, like the pollution in our seas, the state of our rainforests, the fracking issue? Would it be about human trafficking or domestic violence? What is it that breaks your heart? What one thing is calling out to you?

Once you have let yourself feel that call, acknowledge what the issue is. Say it out loud. Write it in your journal, for this is an important clue. It has to do with the meaning of your life, with its value and purpose. Next, think of an activity you love to engage in. What would you do more of if you won the lottery? What are you looking forward to doing when you finally have more time?

Is it golf? Travel? Painting? Writing? Get clear in your mind about the thing that's pulling you. Name it. Speak it. Write it down. These are your creative building blocks. Now, let your heart's desire connect with the thing that breaks your heart and watch what comes from that unlikely marriage. Put the two together, side by side. *Painting/Gaza Strip. Walking/teen suicide. Writing/growing autism rates.* You don't have to do anything about it now, but thoughts may begin to surface that give you some new direction, that marry the two and lead to the birth of a brilliant idea—one that's been knocking on the doors of your imagination but never found an access until now. *When the student is ready, the teacher appears.*

I have never met a person who didn't care about her or his life having value. Who is there to coach us in the matter but our own inner voice? And what is the compass if not joy? Rumi said, *Let yourself be silently drawn by the strange pull of what you really love. It will not lead you astray.* Buddha said, *Engage with joy in all the sorrows of the world.* When we are discerning our next moves, "What do I really want?" is the question we need to ask. It is not "What would Jesus do? What would my mother want me to do? What would my children want?" Trusting our instincts and impulses is key to our success at creating joy and value.

I have seen the world because I love to travel and feel a need to move when I'm up against a wall. If I'm anxious, depressed, at a choice point, bewildered, I make a trip. If I'm at the end of a relationship, the end of my rope, the end of an era, I travel. I try to turn it into something meaningful, but the bottom line is, I'm on the road. I have said goodbye and closed the door on what was. And I set out to meet with whatever will be. Stepping into the unknown comforts me and challenges me. I trust that on the road I will meet my teachers, learn my lessons and be shaken out of whatever trance I'm in. It has never not been the case.

I once started out in my Honda Civic on a cross-country trip through the small towns of America. My mission was to interview people about their values and how they acquired them. Heading south from Syracuse, New York, I was both excited and hesitant at the same time. I kept a yellow legal pad on the passenger seat, adding questions as I thought of them. Before I knew it, I had driven through three states and filled up three pages with questions without having interviewed one person.

When I crossed the Virginia state line, I promised myself I would go into one restaurant and ask to speak with one person at the very least. I drove into a Waffle House parking lot and pumped myself up. I closed my eyes and imagined success. My plan: walk into the restaurant and look around. If someone made eye contact with me, I'd ask if I could interview him or her. I took along a copy of my book, *Making Peace*, for the sake of credibility, and my yellow legal pad with all the questions.

One young man in the back caught my eye when I came through the door. He was wearing a denim jacket and a Playboy baseball cap. He was the only one in the place making eye contact with me. So I approached him, said what I was doing, showed him my book, and asked if he had a few minutes. He nodded and I sat down. When I pulled out my pad of questions and focused in on the first one, I looked right into his eyes and asked, "Where did you get your values from?"

He stared right back at me with a deep, vacuous look. After a few silent moments, he said, with a southern, two-syllable drawl, "Wha-ut?"

I panicked for a second, and then heard a voice in my own head whisper "Go first." Scanning my past for examples, I went first and told the story of how my mother always told me, when I passed a person on the street, to look that person in the eyes, give them a big smile, and say "Hi," as friendly as I could.

I told him it was difficult at first, since I was young and pretty shy when she told me that, but I tried it anyway and kept on doing it. "Eventually it got easier and now" I reported, "I do it all the time, because it's just part of me. So being friendly is one of my values. And I got it from my Mom."

The whole time I talked, he nodded his head and chewed on his toothpick, squinting his eyes so I knew he was with me. When I was done with my story, he asked, "Is it like this? When I was little and my daddy used to whup me when he'd get a drinkin', I'd go out on the back porch wantin' to cry and my Grandaddy would be there. He'd look at me and say, 'Son, looks like you've got some big feelings goin' on. Why don't you get yourself a pad of paper and go down under that oak tree and write yourself some poems. That'll help you with them big feelings.' So I did, I wrote a lot of poems. I still do, when I need to work out my feelings. So I guess that makes me a poet. Is that what you're talkin' about? 'Cause if it weren't for my Grandaddy I never would have got steered in that direction."

I was flabbergasted. I hoped for a ripple and got a tsunami.

"Yes, yes, that's exactly what I'm talking about."

You wanna hear one of my poems?"

He recited a poem by heart, and then wrote it down in my journal. We sat in that red plastic booth for another hour and a half while he told stories he had never told to another person—about his own anger, his big dreams, his pickup truck and double-wide, his drinking problem, his fear of being in love and messing it up like his Dad. And every story he told me lit up my own darkness, taught me something I never knew, and opened me up where I was closed down.

He found parts of himself that had been long lost, simply because I was there to hear and receive them. And the same was true for me. When we left that restaurant, we were two different people from the ones who had walked in. He showed me his tricked out diesel half-ton, then gave me a big hug before I climbed back into my little Honda, alive in a new way.

It had been momentous, that encounter, and what I learned that day that I'll never forget is the magic of "going first." I didn't know, all those years ago, that the word *leadership* comes from an Old English word meaning "go first." It came like a whisper from beyond, a nudging that urged me to open and share so the one I was with felt safe and secure.

My story was a tale of the passing on of values, wrapped in a few paragraphs, a little history, some visual images. And yet, it was powerful enough to break through his walls of silence. Powerful enough to touch what was deep and true inside himself. And from that intimacy and vulnerability that both of us shared, a new story grew, a universal story, the story of *Going First*.

I now know, from that one experience, that uplifting conversations can occur but people count on us going first. Everyone is waiting to be asked. Waiting for someone else to say something real, to share something vulnerable, to set the stage for power talking, for honest revealing.

Since I value such conversations, and rely on them for my joy and sanity, I've been practicing this for many years now, learning more from others' lives than I could from any book. In the process of writing this book together, Ruth and I have delved deeply into each other's lives in an attempt to surface the stories where our wisdom sprouted.

We talk about our childhoods, recalling events where we best learned the meaning of things. We mine the trouble spots, share the sadnesses, confess to the chaos, all in an attempt to harvest whatever treasures can be unearthed, for nothing happens in our lives that is not for our good. The great work for each of us is to master our ordeals and see what blessings are buried in the rubble.

Ruth learned early that creativity helped her deal with a family in turmoil. Drawing and painting became her "safe place." And because she needed to retreat so often to that place in her imagination, her skills in that area grew and grew. As we look back into our younger years, we can see how our experiences happened *for* us as much as *to* us. If we look at it as creators who had something to do with the shaping of our lives, it is possible to give thanks for whatever opportunities allowed us to grow and become whomever we are now. There are no regrets, nor is there anyone to blame—just wonder and amazement at the circuitous routes human beings take to acquire their wisdom and pass it on.

Had we not endured the hardships, mastered the ordeals, processed the pain, we would not be in a position to add much value to the people in our lives. We are confident of our value because we have learned our lessons and have something to offer. We have stories of transformation. We have hit bottom, known despair, lost hope, and we have found our way from there to here. Just as you have, who are sitting with this book in your lap. Look what you have survived. Look at what you know now because of all those adventures. That *knowing* is what gives you value. It is the main gift you have to share, and however it comes out of you is fine. It could be through stories, through social action, through journaling or sports or book club conversations, but the important thing is that it gets expressed. "Not to transmit an experience is to betray it," says Holocaust survivor and writer Elie Wiesel.

EXPANDING THE FRONTIERS OF ART AND CREATIVITY

When we asked in our survey about the beliefs that keep people from expressing their creativity, many admitted that they feel their work has no value. Many more are stopped by the feeling that their work is not good enough and hundreds feel confused about the distinctions between creativity and art.

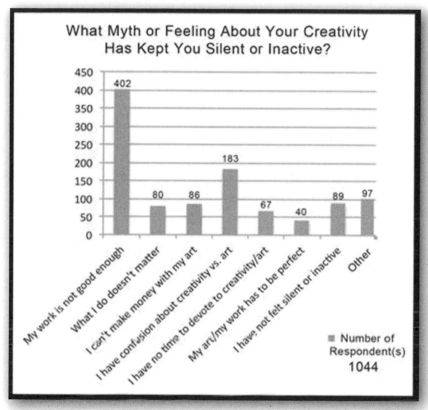

Phillips/Westreich Creativity Study, 2014 (PW003)

Despite the voices that hold us back, we still hunger to push our-selves, to go further with our imaginations, to see what's possible. People want to engage with others, to feel the thrill of creative combustion, the joy of originating new solutions, like spelunkers in a cave, illuminating the unknown.

One of the most revered scientists of all time, Albert Einstein, believed

A human being is a part of the whole, called by us "Universe",
a part limited in time and space. He experiences himself, his
thoughts and feelings as something separated from the rest — a
kind of optical delusion of his consciousness. The striving to free
oneself from this delusion is the one issue of true religion. Not to
nourish the delusion but to try to overcome it is the way to reach
the attainable measure of peace of mind.[5]

Artists and scientists both are discovering and disseminating information that addresses this "optical delusion of separateness." Nobel Peace
Prize nominee physicist Ervin Laszlo cites dozens of research examples
testifying to our intrinsic connectedness in his book *Science and the
Akashic Field*. He quotes physicist David Bohm: "Deep down the consciousness of mankind is one. This is a virtual certainty because even
in the vacuum matter is one; and if we don't see this it's because we
are blinding ourselves to it."Laszlo writes that the brains and minds of
humans are connected by the same information field that links quanta
and galaxies in the universe and cells and organisms in the biosphere.
Particle physicist Henry Stapp believes that consciousness is fundamental to the universe. He writes,

The new physics presents prima facie evidence that our human
thoughts are linked to nature by nonlocal connections: what a
person chooses to do in one region seems immediately to affect
what is true elsewhere in the universe. This nonlocal aspect can
be understood by conceiving the universe to be not a collection
of tiny bits of matter, but rather a growing compendium of 'bits
of information.[6]

On some deep level, we are aware that our choices have an impact on
others, that there is some ineffable connection between our lives and the

lives of our sisters and brothers in the Middle East, North Korea, South Sudan, the West Bank. In all the workshops Ruth and I conduct across the country, people admit to similar feelings. On an interior level, we somehow feel a deep connection to others, yet in the world at large, it is our differences that are reinforced. Personally, for many of us, we sense the inequities and a deep sorrow runs through our nervous systems day and night. Yet we are frozen in our silences, numbed by our distractions, waiting and yearning for war to end, hunger to end, poverty to end.

But these will not end if we remain silent and complacent, if we do not employ our complete creative potential to the imagining of another way. The time has come to be public with our pain, to speak of it, its unbearableness, for it is only then that we begin to address it, to embrace it, and, ultimately, to heal it. Simone Weil once said, "The work of art which I do not make, none other will ever make." The same is true with regard to our cultural contribution. No one else has the same thoughts as I have, the same visions, the same approach to danger, for no one else has lived through what I have lived through, and it is the experiences of our lives that inform our thoughts and actions in the world.

As individuals, the greatest courage that is called for is the courage to be real. When we are real, it releases what is bound, in ourselves and others. It opens the passageways between our hearts and our brains, dissolves the blockages that constrain our imagination, and carries us down to our wellsprings of wisdom. The solutions to our crises are already here. They exist in our relationships, in our stories, in our unfolding forgiveness, and it is through the expression of these things that we will one day live into the answers we seek.

The creativity that is required at this moment in history is a creativity of generosity, of humility, of truth-telling. To create, we need not know the answers. We must only take the questions into our hearts and see what we can make of them. As we have evolved beyond the mechanics and rigidities of the industrial age, so have we evolved into beings who seek more purposeful lives, more inspiring relationships, more creative communities.

To be free to offer the gifts of your heart, to be free of what others might think, to be a truth-teller, a catalyst, a voice in the dark: these are the fruits of the greatest creativity. Creators around the country are using their imaginations to build community and pathways for people to transcend that delusion of consciousness that Einstein refers to. Community-based art programs are increasing as groups of people use the arts to explore pressing social issues.

One vital and successful program is The Social and Public Art Resource Center (SPARC), an organization serving the larger Los Angeles area. From 1974-1975, artist, educator, and UCLA Professor of Chicano/American Studies Judy Baca organized, hired, and trained teams of at-risk youth in the use of mural-making as a cultural tool. Many of them were gang members and part of the justice system, but they learned to tell their stories at a time when there were no Hispanic members on the City Council or the School Board. SPARC strives to give a voice to and celebrate LA's ethnically and economically diverse population. They state on their website:

> SPARC's intent is to examine what we choose to memorialize through public art, to devise and innovate excellent art pieces; and ultimately, to provide empowerment through participatory processes to residents and communities excluded from civic debate. SPARC's works are never simply individually authored endeavors, but rather a collaboration between artists and communities, resulting in art which rises from within the community, rather than being imposed upon it.[7]

SPARC was founded in 1976 by Judy Baca, Filmmaker/Director Donna Deitch, and Artist/Teacher Christina Schlesinger. It was created to amplify the voices of the marginalized in the Los Angeles communities and to provide a new vision of what art could do. Women, people of color, poor and working people, day laborers, youth, and prisoners became the focus in their programming. They believed that art can exist in places where people live and work, and they were focused on a new "public art."

SPARC participants created The Great Wall of Los Angeles, which is one of Los Angeles' true cultural landmarks and one of the country's largest monuments to inter-racial harmony. Its half-mile length (2,754 ft) in the Tujunga Flood Control Channel of the San Fernando Valley hosts thousands of visitors every year, providing a tribute to the working people of California who have shaped its history. Completed over five summers, the Great Wall employed over 400 youth and their families from diverse social and economic backgrounds working with artists, oral historians, ethnologists, scholars, and hundreds of community members.

SPARC has created hundreds of murals throughout the city, hung photographic tapestries in senior citizens centers, and built sculptures for children to play on in vacant lots. They have a deep belief in the value of art in the community and since their beginning, they have been propagating the ideas that art is for everyone regardless of their status in society, that art should not dwell only in rarefied halls but in the places where people live and work, and that the arts can have transformative impact on the most significant social problems of our time.

In an interview for Huffington Post, Judy Baca and Debra Padilla, SPARC's Executive Director since 1991, shared their thoughts on SPARC's evolution and impact.[8] Because they articulate so clearly the role that creativity plays in a healthy, safe community, we are including some of their comments here from an interview with bloggers Julia Wasson and Cathy Weiss:

> **What is the importance of art, especially for children?**
> Judy Baca: I can't remember when art wasn't important. I've told the story about not speaking English, and a great teacher put me in the corner and let me paint. She figured out a way to go directly into my intelligence and make me feel as though I was not totally left out. Then I could talk about my paintings. Arts are a magnificent way to deal with multilingual people. Arts are an entryway.

Once part of process, what's the best way to keep young people involved?

Judy Baca: It doesn't matter if it's art or digging a ditch, building an airplane or making a sculpture, what matters is that it's a creative, innovative act. What really matters is the collaboration and skills young people develop figuring out how to get it done. I had kids who couldn't read or use a ruler, and I'd give them blueprints and say, "Get that up there." And they didn't want to admit they didn't know what a quarter or half inch was. One kid with a long sleeved shirt had hidden the marks of the ruler on his arm, half-inch, quarter-inch, and he could translate the scale, half an inch equals six inches on the wall, so his team wouldn't get behind…Everybody can do something. Some of the young people found in the arts a place to live, but I wasn't intending to make them artists, I wanted to make them citizens, part of the world they lived in.

Debra Padilla, Executive Director of SPARC, had this to say about the value of public arts:

Art has the power to illuminate, interrogate, celebrate and invigorate a moment in time worth remembering, or simply to give a kid who needs one an outlet louder and bigger than his self-doubt.[9]

How does SPARC involve community members?

Community members are why we do what we do. Our *Great Walls Unlimited: Neighborhood Pride Mural Program* painted 105 murals in ethnic neighborhoods in Los Angeles. We hired 95 artists, both emerging and established, and hired 1100-1200 young people as apprentices. We work with schools, churches and local organizations. We want to identify the neighborhoods that could benefit most from having an engaging and lasting public artwork for generations to come. We want to leave something meaningful, the fine quality of art our communities deserve.

Looking for a person to speak with, I called the SPARC Center and had a long conversation with Associate Director, Felipe Sanchez. A bicentennial baby, Felipe was born in 1976, the year that SPARC started. He spoke about the importance of the murals to him as a child in LA. "I remember driving around LA in my teens and seeing the murals from every freeway. They were sacred then, protected by a street code, until the early 2000s when everything changed."[9] The beginning of the 21st century was marked by higher unemployment, a disenfranchised youth culture, city policies that were favoring the corporations and a ban on murals, but according to Sanchez, "it's a new day and a new dawn for muralism in the city."

Although Philadelphia has taken the lead as mural capital of the country, Los Angeles has committed $1.7 million to restore 20 murals and create new ones, due to pressure from the community for socially-relevant public art that reflects its heritage and traditions. As young artists enter the scene, creativity in the mural milieu is expanding exponentially. Muralists are now digitally hand-rendering their designs and painting the whole thing on a Wacom tablet. Once created, the image can be applied on a variety of substrates and enlarged to any size. "We just mounted a mural that was seventy by thirty feet with a resolution of 1000 dots per inch. It's amazing!" said Sanchez.

On the other side of the country, a non-profit in Indianapolis is bringing together people to invigorate public places, create safer neighborhoods, and stir up the community's creative juices. Big Car Collaborative is an artist-led organization that brings art to people and people to art.[10] Its focus is on innovative community-based art that brings people together to make things happen. Their projects create social experiences. It fits into the new category of socially engaged art referred to now as social practice art.

Social Practice Art is a fairly new academic curriculum that attempts to fuse artistry with social activism and community organization. UC

Santa Cruz and California College of the Arts both offer Social Practice programs. Within the Graduate Fine Arts curriculum at California College of the Arts, the Social Practice (SOPR) concentration enables students to immerse themselves in interdisciplinary curriculum. Social practices incorporates art strategies such as urban interventions, guerrilla architecture, "new genre" public art, social sculpture, project-based community practice, interactive media, and street performance.

UC Santa Cruz has a Social Practices Art Research Center embedded within their offerings. Their goal is to have students learn in a multi/interdisciplinary atmosphere fostering project building between artists, scientists, the public and others stakeholders with a shared vision towards active social and environmental change. They hope that their work will support collaborations across various disciplines and create a local, national and global impact.

In a *New York Times* article on the subject, Randy Kennedy writes that many social practice artists "freely blur the lines among object making, performance, political activism, community organizing, environmentalism and investigative journalism, creating a deeply participatory art that often flourishes outside the gallery and museum system. And in so doing, they push an old question — "Why is it art?" [11]

What makes something "art" or not has probably been debated since the first cave drawings. While many museums have largely ignored the new phenomenon, several smaller art institutions see social practice art as a new frontier. The face of activism has changed dramatically since the 60s and 70s, and the number of social issues being addressed by a vast community of cultural creators continues to grow. Activists are using every platform possible to raise the consciousness of the general public which is being programmed 24/7 for massive consumerism.

In Indianapolis, it was consumerism that inspired the name of the Big Car Collaborative. They took their name from a line in a the Robert Creeley poem, *I Know a Man,* "As I said to my friend ... the darkness surrounds us, what can we do against it, or else, shall we & why not, buy a goddamn big car."

Big Car hosted its first social arts show in spring 2005. Though it wasn't hugely attended, it did find Russian visitors dancing to Prince songs and that felt like some kind of success. So Big Car secured the space on a permanent basis and hosted a variety of programs, including art openings on First Fridays, concerts, readings, film screenings and performance art. It helped to establish the venue as a hive of creative activity and with the joint vision and efforts of the Southeast Neighborhood Development (SEND) and artist/entrepreneur Philip Campbell, the former G.C. Murphy department store was converted into a gathering place for all things visual art.

The Big Car social artists later began working as part of a city-wide socially engaged project, with collaborators working as embedded artists at the table for city-wide initiatives. In Lafayette, Indiana, they initiated a three-phase program. Phase 1 was *Exploring and Learning*. Artists from the neighborhood photograph and map the area, attend meetings, research history and demographics. They also meet with residents of the area and listen to their hopes and wishes for the neighborhood.

In Phase Two, *Giving and Demonstrating*, they give the neighborhood gifts of graphic design, marketing support, and whatever skills they have to offer. Once they are part of the neighborhood's leadership team, they contribute to the planning process with input and ideas. Using tools that they refer to as "tactical urbanism," the artists help others see how their ideas are moving from abstract to concrete, how the people are actually co-creating the community of their dreams.

In this phase, Big Car collaborators create bonds with people by doing physical work together. This builds trust and connections that meeting and talking can never build.

Phase Three, *Making and Sustaining*, involves a larger collaboration among residents, stakeholders, local and out-of-town artists and other cultural partners who commit to using art and culture as a way to strengthen their community.

In a partnership with the City of Indianapolis and Downtown Indy, the Big Car Collaborative launched a ten week initiative called *Spark:*

Monument Circle in July 2015. Seven days a week, they facilitated creative programming and visitor experiences for people to enjoy interactive art, history experiences, yoga, guided walks, talks and play experiences for all ages. They posted on their website the menu of activities that city residents could choose from day by day. Here is an example of their offerings;

During the run of Spark, these events happened each day from 11 a.m. to 8 p.m.:

Mellow Mondays encourage low-tech, relaxing experiences ... with the Indianapolis Public Library's Bookmobile, lunchtime yoga, and live ambient music.

Talking Tuesdays feature the "Ask an Expert" desk, conversation prompts, and a Listening Booth.

Walking Wednesdays are days when people meet to walk and talk and take organized, artist/expert-led walks from the Circle to other destinations nearby — and fitness walks, too.

Throwback Thursdays focus on history – especially of Monument Circle – and bringing history to life with four characters: Gov. Oliver Morton, city planner Alexander Ralston, entrepreneur John Freeman, and First Lady Esther Ray Brown.

Phono Fridays feature music, sound, and DJs – including crowd-sourced, vinyl, spoken word

Social Saturdays feature morning workouts, open call and community events, and a themed procession each week.

Cycle Sundays include opportunities for bike riders.

Their website lists an array of past, present and future projects that would spark the imagination of any community-minded citizen looking for ideas to create a safer, friendlier neighborhood.

The binding material of social practice is person-to-person exchange, interaction, or participation. These situations, organizations and events can involve various media including photography, video, drawing, text, sound, sculpture, political art, design, eco-art and performance art. The Social Practices Art Network (SPAN) is a media resource for individuals, organizations, community groups and institutions that are interested in new genre arts forms and practices [12] It is an exciting platform and virtual billboard for a number of valuable and cutting edge projects being designed by artistic innovators who are taking the culture into their own hands.

Another impressive group that is connecting the dots between the arts and social justice is *Creative Time*, a New York City based organization that collaborates with artists and others to present ambitious art projects in public spaces.[13] *Creative Time* commissions, produces, and presents work that challenges the status quo, catalyzes civic involvement, and inspires people to look at the world in new ways. *Creative Time* projects have incorporated the ideas of hundreds of artists, cultural producers, and social-justice advocates, including art world luminaries, rural community organizers, and international activists.

Creative Time was established at a seminal moment in the history of art, when artists were exploring new forms and mediums that took their works beyond the confines of galleries and other traditional exhibition spaces and into the public sphere. The concept for the organization emerged in 1973, during an informal discussion among three friends in New York City: Karin Bacon and Susan Henshaw Jones, who worked in Mayor Lindsay's administration, and actress and dancer Anita Contini, who would become *Creative Time*'s first executive director.

In an effort to revitalize the South Street Seaport area, the three women organized a summer arts festival that brought together two rarely intersecting communities: the artists who lived in the neighborhood and the business people who worked there. *Creative Time* soon became known as the leading facilitator of experimental public art in New York, and its initiatives were viewed as a way to improve life in the City. Their work is guided by three core values: art matters, artists' voices are important in shaping society, and public spaces are places for creative and free expression.

The group has a distinguished record of trailblazing projects that engage diverse audiences and issues, foster new ideas and artistic innovation, and reimagine public spaces. A visit to their website is well worth the time, as it presents a litany of contemporary responses to questions about the changing face of activism. In recent years, the organization has expanded its programming beyond New York City to locations across the country, including New Orleans, Los Angeles, Miami, and, through its Global Residency Program, throughout the globe.

In 2009, the first global summit was held in the New York Public Library. It provided a major venue where people working at the convergence of art and social justice could share their work and start to establish relationships with a like minded community. The summit has since grown into a leading conference where presenters and audience members meet and collaborate on strategies for changing our world through art.

Their 2013 summit explored how art and social justice should be connected. A *New York Times* article proclaimed the event as "visionary." The conference gets over 5,000 live attendees and thousands more who watch via Livestream or at one of the 70+ international Screening Sites. The 2015 summit was in Vienna with a focus on knowledge: how it is produced and how it comes into contact with civil society. The list of presenters is a clear indicator of its commitment to diversity, as the faculty represents artists and educators from all over the world. Exploring the integration of art and politics is a critical part of the agenda, as is furthering the conversation about creativity and culture-making.

A SIGN OF OUR TIME

That organizations like SPARC, Big Car and Creative Time have risen up at this time in history is a sign that we are evolving into a more democratized understanding of our role as cultural creators. These organizations are calling forth the creativity of the public in imaginative ways. They are creating new opportunities for public art, public conversation, public gatherings around common issues where people can find each other, have meaningful conversations with each other. They are stimulating dialogue among diverse groups that may very well lead to a newness of vision, a newfound hope, new avenues for expression in the imaginations of hundreds of people.

Whatever any one of us creates, if we put something into the world that has our thumbprint of hope on it, it will add value to someone, somewhere. A Balinese dancer once wrote, "There's someone out there who needs you. You must live your life so that person can find you." When I read those words, my life suddenly changed. My whole relationship to marketing changed. My question shifted from "Will they like this?" to "How can I get my work to them? They need it."

Ruth and I create all day long—we create relationships of consequence, cutting edge organizations, inspiring events, photographs, jewelry, mixed-media and music. When we enter the studio, it is quieter, inner focused, healing and meditative. When we enter the marketplace, it is frenzied, ever-demanding, outer focused. In both situations, we are listening deeply and responding intuitively. We are in touch with the heartbeat of the Earth, of the global citizenry. We care deeply and we act always.

There is rarely a measurement for the reach of our work. Creators are not gifted with immediate gratification. We create and we share our creations. It is that act that heals us, and that act we hope will help heal the world. This is our trust, our faith. This is the gesture of our deep love for the world in which we live.

CHAPTER 3

LISTEN UP: WHY A MINDFULNESS PRACTICE IS MAGICAL

*Spiritual" is not necessarily religion. A spiritual impulse draws
a person towards inner meaning, toward the intangible, toward
the enhancement of consciousness and the search to serve the
dignity of mankind.*
JACOB NEEDLEMAN

THE REWARDS OF MINDFULNESS

DURING A TALK to thousands of scientists on the subject of neuroscience and meditation, the Dalai Lama admitted that meditating is hard work for him even though he does it for four hours every morning. He said if scientists were able to put electrodes in his brain and provide him with the same outcome as he gets from meditating, he would gladly volunteer.[1]

If one of our great world leaders dedicates four hours a day to something that he describes as "hard work," there has to be a pretty significant payoff, it would seem. And based on the latest scientific research into meditation, it's easy to see what that payoff is. Dr. Andrew Newberg is a neuroscientist who studies the relationship between brain function and various mental states, using brain imaging techniques such as SPECT (single-photon emission computed tomography), fMRI (Functional magnetic resonance imaging), and EEG (electroencephalogram). A pioneer in the neurological study of spiritual experiences, his research indicates that the human brain is already hardwired for enlightenment. Over millions of years of evolution, we have been preparing ourselves for the experience of oneness with the cosmos, and now, through mindfulness practices, dedicated meditators are experiencing just that [2]. Newberg calls this state Absolute Unitary Being, the ultimate unitary state.

He likens this state to mysticism, which he refers to as the art of establishing conscious relation with the Absolute. He writes:

> Mystical experience is not about magic, or mind-reading, or the conjuring of visions or spirits; it is nothing more or less than an uplifting sense of genuine spiritual union with something larger than the self... At the heart of all the mystics' descriptions . . . is the compelling conviction that they have risen above material existence, and have spiritually united with the absolute. The primordial longing for this absolute union, and the transcendent experiences to which it might lead, are the common threads that run through the mystical traditions of East and West, of ancient centuries, and of the present...The attainment of spiritual union through detachment from the self . . . is rooted in something deeper and more primal than theology or scriptural revelation. . . . those mechanics are wired into the human brain, and are set in motion by nothing more tangible than the mind willing itself toward God.[3]

This is most likely the kind of "outcome" the Dalai Lama was referring to when he spoke of the results of his meditation. Buddhists are after that sense of oneness, that awareness that nothing is separate from the One Thing. When Newberg studied eight Tibetan Buddhist practitioners using SPECT scan, he discovered that when a meditator withdraws from the outside world, a shift occurs in the brain activity from the parietal lobes (where we experience a distinction between our self and the world) to the frontal lobes (where the sense of separateness disappears and the self perceives its oneness with the world.) The process of awakening is more a function of the brain in a meditative state than a result of a psychological or philosophical shift, according to Newberg's research. It is a biological process, brought on by a shift in the brain that causes our sense of separateness to be replaced by an experience of absolute oneness.

So what's required of us for enlightenment? Meditation. A mindfulness practice. A commitment of time each day to withdraw from the world's chaos and settle in to our body's deep calm. It's that commitment of time that is the hard part— along with the sitting still, the surrender to mindlessness, to the observation of nothing but our own breathing.

Meditation requires no faith or memorized prayers. It doesn't depend on a notion of God, or a feeling of channeling, or a quest for awakening. It is a state of being present. Really present. Aware of your thoughts, your breath, your ability to move from thinking to non-thinking. It is separate from religion, as the sea is separate from the shore. According to the spiritual teacher Jiddu Krishnamurti, "True spiritual practice springs *from*, not toward, enlightenment. Our practice does not lead to unity consciousness—it *is* unity consciousness."

It is the space and place where you love yourself—honor, heal, and collect yourself. Where you hear the knock of wisdom and open your arms to it. It is a time when mystery trumps certainty, when the half-gods go and the Real arrives. Without it, we are like a bulb without a filament, a plate of empty calories, an artesian well without a tap. With no place to refuel, we are stuck on empty.

Mindfulness meditation is a retraining of the mind by the mind. It is the cultivation of new thought patterns and new mental behaviors that liberate us from our addictions to dualistic thinking and conditioned reactions. While there is pain in our lives that is unavoidable, there is a certain amount of suffering that we create for ourselves, because of our attitudes, our false perceptions, our prejudices. Mindfulness sweeps over the mental landscape and clears it of those mines that could explode into thought disasters if we're not cautious or conscious.

Research studies are providing evidence that meditation techniques can lead to more creative thinking. At Leiden University in the Netherlands, cognitive psychologists Lorenza Colzato and Dominique Lippelt had 40 individuals meditate for 25 minutes before doing thinking tasks. There were both experienced meditators and people who were meditating for the first time. The scientists found that after Open Monitoring meditation, where participants were receptive to every thought and sensation, they achieved better results in divergent thinking.[4]

There are hundreds of peer-reviewed scientific papers offering evidence that mindfulness improves mental and physical wellbeing while also enhancing creativity and decision making. In short, mindfulness is a potent antidote to anxiety, stress, depression, exhaustion and irritability. Regular meditators are not only happier and more contented, but they are far less likely to suffer from psychological distress as well. [5]

As creators, there is a great advantage in mastering our own thoughts, in knowing how to hunker down into our own calm core. When we have the sinking feeling we are not good enough, we can remember that is part of our cultural programming. Most of us have not been conditioned for confidence. Being mindful of this, we can shift gears and rethink: I am here to create beauty, joy, value, and I will be true to that mission. When we become anxious about the future or regretful about the past, we can burrow into the present, find our balance, get centered and get on with our work. This is what a mindfulness practice helps one do.

It is a move toward mental autonomy, away from inherited thoughts and into our own originality. Mindfulness is self-organized consciousness, self-supporting thought. What feels like stepping out is also a stepping in—to higher dimensions of being, knowing, feeling. It is an experience of bliss, which is a state of calm and perfect groundedness. It is the bass to joy's treble, the basement to joy's rooftop. When Joseph Campbell urged people to "follow their bliss," I don't think he was talking about living as if you've won the lottery. I don't think he was speaking of ecstasy as we know it in the common vernacular, but rather of the ecstasy that comes from the Latin *extasis*, or out of the static. And this is where mindfulness takes us: out of the static.

It roots us in a place of calm so we can navigate through our days peacefully, without thinking that things should be happening differently.

It opens doors to the inner voice that is rarely heard in the clamor and chaos. Mindfulness creates a place where the wisdom in our cells gets to see the light of day. It's the place where fears disappear, where the majesty of the present trumps the meagerness of the past.

Ruth writes about her experience with yoga:

> Three days a week I have a yoga instructor come to my home and we do yoga together. Yes, I could go to a yoga class or I could do yoga to a video, or just do it on my own. But I know me. I can find dozens of reasons not to do yoga today. I have two paintings in my studio that I would love to be working on. My mind is racing with ideas as to how to proceed with the next layer for each piece. I could work on my PowerPoint presentation for the next lecture I am giving. I can be thinking about a strategy for any number of groups I am involved with, but that is not the same as a mindfulness practice just for me that supports my mind, my body and my spirit all at the same time.
>
> When I first started doing yoga about 5 years ago after a lifetime of marathon aerobics, running, pilates and gyrotonics, I began to feel the effects of overworking my physical body and not paying much attention to my mind and my spirit. Doing the work I do with my foundation, I knew of yoga and the benefits heralded by so many for so long, but I couldn't quite see how it might help me. I gave up the running and aerobics looking for something that would sustain me well into my old age, so I thought I would try Yoga. For anyone who has started Yoga, it is contrary to everything we are taught to do in the Western society. Yoga is solitary. It is meditative. It is personal, and you are not competing with anyone. It is just you, the poses and the mat.
>
> After beginning Yoga, first thing out of the gate, I strained almost every muscle in my body because it wasn't used to stretching and lengthening. I was competing with myself. I laid out

what I thought my body was capable of doing and proceeded to compete with myself. Wrong. I was agitated and angry with myself because I wanted to do it perfectly, and my body, mind and spirit weren't cooperating.

I was taught by a very smart group of people to 'fake it until you make it'. Keep showing up and doing the work until you finally want to show up, so I did. Months and months went by and I couldn't see any improvement in my flexibility. I didn't look forward to it but kept showing up because I wanted to do this. Old people can do Yoga. I wanted that for me. But I have a tendency to multi-task. So I would do my Yoga and think about a painting process I was working on, what I wanted to accomplish during the day, just any number of things.

Well, in order to do Yoga, you have to give it your complete, undivided attention in that moment. You must be fully present, in the zone and breathing. If you are not, you fall over. You can't balance and many of the poses require balance. I don't exactly remember when it happened for me, but one day I came in to do my Yoga, felt fully present, noticed my body was working on its own without me pressing and pushing. And I felt centered and really enjoyed it. I had 'made it'. Now I look forward to it and if I have to miss for some reason I feel that something in my day is missing. Is every day the same? No.

Some days no matter how present I try to be, I don't have good balance. If the barometric pressure changes, I can feel it in my joints and I don't have the range of motion but I still show up because 5,000 years of Asian Medicine can't be wrong.

PIONEERING MINDFULNESS IN THE WEST

Since 1979, when molecular biologist Dr. Jon Kabat-Zinn, son of a painter and a biomedical scientist, developed the Mindfulness-Based Stress Reduction Clinic in Massachusetts, mindfulness meditation practice has become a way of life for thousands of people. He recruited chronically ill patients not responding well to traditional treatments and offered them an eight-week stress reduction program, incorporating meditation techniques, yoga, mindfulness practices. His program was referred to as Mindfulness Based Stress Reduction (MBSR), and studies have found that pain-related drug use was decreased, energy levels heightened, and feelings of self esteem increased for a majority of participants.

Kabat-Zinn's MBSR began to get increasing notice with the publication of his first book, *Full Catastrophe Living: Using the Wisdom of Your Body and Mind to Face Stress, Pain, and Illness* which gave detailed instructions for the practice. Then, in 1993, his work in the Stress Reduction Clinic was featured in Bill Moyers's PBS special *Healing and the Mind*, generating more public interest in mindfulness. Since then, many MBSR clinics have opened, either as standalone centers or as part of a hospital's holistic medicine program, and more than 20,000 people have taken advantage of the training.

According to their website, mindfulness practice is ideal for cultivating greater awareness of the unity of mind and body, as well as of the ways the unconscious thoughts, feelings, and behaviors can undermine emotional, physical, and spiritual health.[6] The mind is known to be a factor in stress-related disorders, and meditation has been shown to have a positive effect, such as lowering blood pressure and reducing overall stress and emotional reactivity. MBSR also uses yoga to help reverse the disuse atrophy that occurs in people who do not exercise, especially for those with pain and chronic illnesses. They are currently exploring the physiological benefits of MBSR in people who have had significant impairment in cardiac function following a heart attack.

Because the programs describe meditation practice in such easy-to-understand terms, and because the research results are so positive, there is a fast-growing movement of mindfulness into mainstream institutions such as medicine, health care and hospitals, schools, higher education, corporations, prisons, the legal profession, and professional sports. There are dozens of online courses offered around the country, a mindfulness without borders.org, drop in meditation centers, and a myriad of mindfulness apps for every smart phone. My own alma mater, Syracuse University, offers a free eight week course at the campus counseling center.

Mindfulness is an act of self-healing. It is moment to moment awareness. It is being fully awake, fully present for the moments of our lives, without striving or judging. A mindfulness practice is a symbol of our reverence for our own lives. It is accessible to everyone for free. If you think you don't have time for a mindfulness practice, you are probably not committed to an extraordinary life, which is fine. That's your choice. You should simply be aware you are making it. The poet Colin Wilson once said, "Turning on the light is easy if you know where the switch is." Some people think of mindfulness as their switch. With it comes illumination, a lightening up of spirit.

I was on my way to my writing room this morning, determined that nothing would get in the way of me churning out a chapter or two. I was committed and joyful, looking forward to the newness that comes with the creative process—the surprising phrases, the keen metaphors, the unabashed ideas that surprise me as they prance onto the page. When the doorbell rang, I said a happy hello to the young man with the package, signing my name on the dotted line.

There was a book by poet/writer Mark Doty in the envelope, *Still Life with Oysters and Lemon,* sent to me by a friend in New Jersey. I thought of the quote from Katherine Paterson, the writer, who wrote, "As I look back on what I have written, I can see that the very persons who have taken away my time are those who have given me something to say." I wondered if Mark Doty might be in this category.

I wasn't trying to distract myself. I was actually eager to write. But the book was short. I was seduced. "There has to be a reason this arrived right now," I said to myself as I detoured into my bedroom, sprawling out on the bed and opening to the first page.

Within a few pages, I knew exactly what Paterson was talking about. Mark's insights and perspectives about the power of still-life paintings were breathtaking. He was writing about the same thing I was setting out to write about: the impact of our original thoughts, our creative works on the world around us. Our thoughts, our words, our creations are all like tiny picture puzzle pieces making up the world we live in. I come with my pieces. You come with yours. We put them together and cultures take shape.

Our cities and towns look like they look because we live in them. We contribute or we don't. We leave tracks of our lives, or we don't. People glibly announce "there is nothing new under the sun," but never in human history has there been such a proliferation of new ideas, new technologies, new discoveries. We have never been so closely connected to each other so intimately and immediately.

The planet itself seems to be rewiring its neural networks through the work of our brains, our hands, and our hearts. As we each acknowledge our role as creator and begin to use our thoughts and words as a painter uses paints and brushes, we step up the pace of our own evolution. With our commitment to progress comes progress. With our dedication to creativity comes inspiration.

CREATIVITY TAKEN IN AGGREGATE

Mark Doty writes that "when we describe the world we come closer to saying who we are." In our poems, our daily work, our stories, what we are revealing is something deep and unique to us. Some of my poems might have been written in the Middle Ages, but there are a few that have come straight from the future, handed down through some cosmic conduit. The more one creates, the better one understands the nature of creativity—its mystery, its magic and alchemy. To dedicated creators, there is often a feeling of surprise, of exchange and intimacy with an invisible force. It is as if two worlds have come together—the physical and metaphysical—in the service of truth and beauty. Our most original and honest works carry an essence that is essentially un-nameable. There is a power there, a force or energy that stays with the work even upon our death. It belongs to the work. It is the spirit of the work. It is what sustains it.

Doty writes about an evening he was having dinner with friends and was seated in front of a still life. "I was seated with my back to the painting, but I felt its magnetism; I was trying to converse, I was conversing, but I felt still its pull." He writes about the capacity of the objects to carry meaning; that the objects depicted are soulful, suffused with intimacy, anything but lifeless. He writes of Louise Gluck's assertion that "poetry is autobiography stripped of context and commentary," and suggests that the statement is "true of still life as well—how else could these few things on the table before us, arrayed against the dark, glow with such a fierce warmth?'

Our entire histories go into each creation though our renderings contain only what can be seen or read or heard, perceived through the threshold of the viewers' senses. As Doty so poignantly puts it:

Where there was a person, a voice, a range and welter of experience compressed into lines and images, now there are only lines and images. Where there was a life, now there is form. And the form, spoken, breathes something of that life out into the world again. It restores a human presence; hidden in the lines, if they are good lines, is the writer's breath, are the turns of thought and of phrase, the habits of saying, which makes those words unmistakable. And so the result is a permanent intimacy; we are brought into relation with the perceptual character, the speaking voice, of someone we probably never knew, someone no one can know now, except in this way. [7]

My mother died recently, and in her belongings I found a poem written by my father in 1943. It was published in the *Black River Journal*, in response to a letter to the editor criticizing farm boys for not joining the war effort. As it turned out, my father tried to enlist but was rejected because he was a farmer and the country needed the fruits of his labor. Where there was once his life, his desire to wear a uniform, his willingness to fight, there is now this form, these lines, the spirit of him still breathing. These are his hand-written words, still alive:

In answer to: Win the War 1943

I read your letter with much concern
And then decided that it was my turn
To explain to you and others as well
The importance of farm boys—all in a shell.

In my opinion, it was your thought
That some of the farm boys are easily bought.
Now I don't think you know the way we feel
And that's just what I'm about to reveal.

It wasn't our choice to do as we please
Or didn't you ever hear of the word "freeze."
I know of hundreds who tried to enlist
But the draft board had orders and had to resist.

I don't think that you can mention a one
That isn't willing to shoulder a gun
What would you do if we all did this?
Run the farms by hit and miss.

You mentioned the cow, as a good place to hide
But I'll inform you, that we still have pride
You think of a farm as just a cow;
That's just the half of it, I'll tell you right now.

It all looks simple to folks like you
But you've still got to eat, to see the war through.
Now I don't pretend to be a famed poet
But just a farm boy, and I want you to know it.

My father did not have a mindfulness practice that I know of, but he favored silence over everything. On our long rides through the country, he rarely spoke. We never played music in the house when he was there. When he did his chores, cleaned the gutters, spread the hay, milked the cows, he was alone with his thoughts, and happy. If he didn't have something important to say, he said nothing.

And when he did speak, it mattered, like this poem matters. His words were clean, clear, concise. They revealed his feelings, but most subtly. My mother said it broke his heart that he couldn't enlist, but you can't see that in the poem. You see acceptance and resolve, but not his pain. He somehow mastered that.

Clarissa Pinkola Estes, author of *Women Who Run With the Wolves*, writes:

> Ours is not the task of fixing the entire world all at once, but of stretching out to mend the part of the world that is within our reach. Any small, calm thing that one soul can do to help another soul, to assist some portion of this poor suffering world, will help immensely. One of the most calming and powerful actions you can do to intervene in a stormy world is to stand up and show your soul.[8]

That's what my father did. He stood up and showed his soul.

Artists are the ones who make the invisible visible, who give words and colors and sounds and shapes to the human adventure. They portray it in such a way that we understand more clearly who we are, how we are connected. Italian poet and Nobel Prize winner Salvatore Quasimodo said that "poetry is the revelation of a feeling that the poet believes to be interior and personal but which the reader recognizes as his own." Poetry, like all the arts, helps us find ourselves. It directs us inward, points us to our essence. It is neither feminine nor masculine, but the perfect blending of the two. It is where the wild wooliness of our physical being joins with the deep holiness of our spiritual being, giving birth to a new entity that expands the magic and meaning of both. Poetry awakens the imagination, stimulates the intellect, stirs the deep waters of our intuition—opening new doors to originality in thought and action.

Mindfulness is the road that gets us there. The process of paying attention to our thoughts and assessing them for authenticity is important work for any creator. It is a rigorous discipline, a meticulous undoing of old habits. It requires the capacity to not simply withstand the tension of opposites, but to become the mechanism for their transformation. Just as a battery cable needs to be connected to the positive and negative poles to give it the power to recharge a dead battery, so it is with us. If we learn to bring the opposites together in our own lives—to welcome ideas that differ, to embrace people from different cultures and creeds—then we learn the alchemy of creation. We become practitioners in the art of generating power—authentic, renewable, and renewing power.

It is this generous gift of our essence, this soul-sharing that attracts others to our light. It is our speaking out that calls forth the co-creators we are looking for. Just as the beauty of a rose summons the bee when it is time for pollination, so does the beauty of our soul summon our kindred spirits when we dare to bare it. There is nothing more luminous and alluring than the human soul, and nowhere does it shine as clearly as it shines in the process of self-revelation. We are relational beings and we come to understand ourselves precisely in the context of our relationships.

When you share your fears with me, your joys or brokenness, you give me a way to better understand my own. Your speaking is a mirror in which I find myself. That is the gift of our self-expression. When we give shape to our interior world, put words to it, offer it to others, we are offering more than the eye can see. This is why our creative work is so essential. It is not pointless or foolhardy. It is an act of faith, an act of kindness, crucial to our own healing and the healing of the planet.

In our world today, there is a great opening for voices that can unify, words that can weave our tattered pieces back into their original oneness. It is a creative endeavor that involves as much spirit as thought and calls for a most illuminated imagination, which exists right now in the center of each of us. It may be sluggish from disuse, or enshrouded in fear or doubt, but it is there, waiting to be rediscovered and deployed into service. And what is it that brings our imaginations back to life? What is it that lures our creativity out of its hibernating state? It is a sense that somehow it matters what we do or say.

The socio-political transformation we are now undergoing is actuated by the push of our global dilemmas and the pull of a vision of what could be. It is that very tension between what is and what could be that is causing an eruption of evolved thinking. Just as technology has changed our ways of doing business, so has it altered our perception of reality. People are beginning to think and feel in non-linear ways and brain research is showing us how and why this is happening.

MINDFULNESS BENEFITS IN HEALTH

Some researchers have concluded that it is possible to master our brainwaves through meditation and therapeutic techniques, and that doing so can result in healing from sickness, entering creative states at will, opening one's gates to deeper intuition, and improving interpersonal relationships. We are evolving to a point where we can work with our own brainwaves to cause higher levels of consciousness and more effective self-healing. In her book, *The High Performance Mind: Mastering Brainwaves for Insight, Healing, and Creativity*, psychologist and neurotherapist Anna Wise outlines techniques that can help to "awaken" the mind and lead to a high-performance life.[9]

She writes:

The awakened mind is clearer, sharper, quicker and more flexible than ordinary states. Thinking feels fluid rather than rigid. Emotions become more available and understandable, easier to work with and transform. Information flows more easily between the conscious, subconscious, and unconscious levels. Intuition, insight and empathy increase and become more integrated into normal consciousness. With an awakened mind, it becomes easier to visualize and imagine, and to apply this increased imagination to one's creative process in many areas. As a result of all this, one has a greater feeling of choice, freedom and spiritual awareness.[10]

Everything we experience passes through our filter of conditioning and beliefs which actually determine the reality we experience. Many people are still operating with belief systems that were handed down to them when they were children. They have not thought to question their beliefs because they have never taken the time to become aware of their beliefs and actually choose which ones to keep or let go. A meditation practice commonly leads to a re-evaluation of our childhood programming. It offers us time and space to actually see and review our thoughts as they pass through. Once we realize which belief systems dominate our lives, we can choose then to replace them or not.

Elkhonon Goldberg, Ph.D., is a scientist, educator, and clinician, renowned for his work in neuropsychology and cognitive neuroscience. He is a Clinical Professor of Neurology at New York University School of Medicine and writes about the ways we can use our brains to create the reality we want. According to Goldberg,

> The frontal lobes possess the mechanism which can liberate the organism from the past and project itself into the future. The frontal lobes equip the organism with the ability to create neural models of something that does not exist yet but something which you want to exist. These inner models can then be projected by the frontal lobes into the future where they are going to materialize in the outer, physical world as your reality. [11]

The formula is this: when you want to create something, get an image of what you want in your mind and that image will serve as a kind of blueprint for the ultimate creation. According to brain researcher Erik

Hoffmann, the blueprint actually "attracts and directs the energy, so the creation finally manifests on the physical level. This means that you attract the things and situations you most believe in."[12] The physical world we encounter is actually a reflection of our beliefs.

Changing our beliefs so that we can change our reality is one of the most creative acts of our life. A mindfulness practice can lead to a feeling that life is happening *through* us, not *to* us. Even if our practice is only ten or fifteen minutes a day, it is enough to cause a shift in our thinking and open up opportunities for evolutionary change.

Universal intelligence is coursing through us as it courses through every atom in every cell. It is the source of our inspiration. As the writer Doris Lessing once said, "I didn't have a thought. There was a thought around." All of our inventions and creations come from this intelligence, which is the same force that causes the seed to burst through its husk and journey upward in search of the light. Constant change, constant progress, constant adaptation. It is the nature of being. And while it is thought provoking and stimulating to some, to others it is a source of anxiety and stress.

James S. Gordon, MD, is a Harvard-trained psychiatrist and pioneer in Integrative Medicine who is Founder and Director of The Center for Mind-Body Medicine in Washington, DC. He uses his mind-body medicine techniques to help heal depression, anxiety and psychological trauma. His programs teach self-awareness and self-care to health professionals around the world, including those in traumatized communities in the greatest need. He has worked in Kosovo, Gaza, Israel, New Orleans, Haiti, and with 9/11 NYC firefighters and families. He does ongoing work with the U.S. military. Jim and his team combine modern science, wisdom traditions, and human connection to create powerful new programs on a simple concept–self-care.

We know from research that 80% of all illnesses are related to chronic stress. Numerous studies have demonstrated that mind-body medicine techniques lower blood pressure and stress hormone levels, relieve pain, improve immune functioning, and improve clinical conditions such as HIV, cancer, insomnia, anxiety, depression and post traumatic stress disorder (PTSD). Gordon's Mind-Body Medicine program focuses on the interactions between mind and body and the powerful ways in which emotional, mental, social and spiritual factors directly affect health. The scientifically-validated techniques the Center teaches enhance each person's capacity for self-care and self-awareness. These techniques include meditation, guided imagery, mindful eating, biofeedback, and the use of drawings, journals and movement to express thoughts and feelings. Self-care, self-awareness and self-expression are a holy trinity.

In Gordon's program, the use of mind-body skills reduced PTSD symptoms, depression and feelings of hopelessness in Palestinian children and adolescents. A research study showed that the groundbreaking model can be used to produce lasting changes in post traumatic stress symptoms including flashbacks, nightmares, withdrawal and numbing in highly traumatized children. The work proved valuable among children who lived in an area of Kosovo where 90% of the homes were burned and bombed and 20% of the children lost one or both parents. Because of their success rate, the Department of Defense has awarded the Center a grant to study the effects of mind-body skills groups on veterans returning from Afghanistan and Iraq.

Another program making national waves is the Center for Mindfulness at the University of San Diego. Dr. Steven Hickman is a Licensed Clinical Psychologist and Founder/Director of the UCSD Center for Mindfulness, a program of community building, clinical care, professional training and research. His Mindful Self Compassion (MSC) program advocates for self-compassion as an essential aspect of a mindful life. Research has shown that self-compassion enhances emotional wellbeing, boosts happiness, reduces anxiety and depression, and helps maintain healthy habits such as diet and exercise. Being both mindful and compassionate leads to greater ease and well-being in our daily lives.

A typical MSC group consists of 10–25 participants and, depending on the size of the group, one or two teachers. Since group participants are likely to encounter uncomfortable emotions, at least one teacher is a trained mental health professional. MSC co-leaders teach by modeling— by embodying compassion and self-compassion. Teachers also encourage participants to support one another by sharing their own experiences. The purpose of the course is to develop a level of self-compassion that helps people navigate ordinary difficulties as they arise in their lives.

Today, there are dozens of programs available for people who want to live a more authentic, grounded life. The UCSD Center for Mindfulness offers a Self-Compassion test on their website.[13] No matter where you are, you can Google mindfulness or MBSR and you will find a resource near you to help keep you on the path. The road to self compassion and mindfulness is a personal journey that begins with the first step. It doesn't matter when you take it, but it does matter that you take it, if you hunger for a life that has ease, joy and purpose to it.

Mindfulness as a practice can be approached in as many ways as there are people practicing it. There is no right way, no way to fail if you are truly committed. We have supplied a lot of examples here as a way of showing that the "idea" of mindfulness has reached critical mass. From both a scientific and spiritual perspective, all the evidence is in to support meditation as an important element in creating a life of balance and value.

There is no proof that you need a mindfulness practice to succeed, but there is plenty of evidence that shows a practice of mindfulness commonly leads to higher creativity, better health, deeper self-awareness. I have friends who started out with a commitment of three minutes a day. That was all they were able to carve out from their busy lives. But they were committed to those three minutes. They removed themselves from the world's frenzy every day for that brief respite into silence and solitude. And that quiet cavern of calm changed their lives.

Now they have increased their time of quiet, taken full possession of their lives, slowed down to a manageable speed and begun the projects they could never begin before. It may seem like a leap of faith, an impossible dream, a reward you don't feel worthy of—but, whatever the obstacles, you can dissolve them today. You can choose health, choose happiness, choose your self. You can start today with as little time as you can manage. It will grow, I promise. You will change. Your life will change. And the creator that you are will begin to thrive.

Why not give it a whirl? You have nothing to lose but your stress.

CHAPTER 4

CREATING TIME: WHY TIME ISN'T A PROBLEM
UNLESS YOU THINK IT IS

Time is a man-made construct. If you need more, make more.
DEEPAK CHOPRA

ALL WE HAVE

WE HAVE A funny relationship with time. We treasure it, like we treasure money, yet we hesitate to spend it on ourselves. We complain that we can't make our time go around, yet day after day we spend what time we have on things we don't want to be doing. When asked about solitude or a spiritual practice, people commonly say "I don't have time for those."

Oddly enough, time is one of the few things we *do* have. It's actually *all* we have. We're born. We have time. We die. So what we do with that time is in *our* hands. In *The Tibetan Book of Living and Dying,* Buddhist meditation master Sogyal Rinpoche writes of our tendency to fill up our whole lives with petty projects and never get to the real questions, like why are we here and what are we doing with our lives?

He calls it "active laziness" and describes both Eastern and Western manifestations of it. In the East, it consists of lounging around all day in the sun, drinking tea, gossiping with friends, and listening to music blaring on the radio. In the West, he writes, it consists of "cramming our lives with compulsive activity, so that there is no time at all to confront the real issues."

When it comes to making time for creative projects—projects that are fun, imaginative, life affirming, mood altering, and spiritually nourishing—we're hard pressed to justify our choices. It sometimes feels "selfish" when we put others' needs aside and tend to our own. If we're simply creating for the joy of it, or for the many ways it heals and inspires us, we often have to deal with negative voices that chastise that behavior.

Time has become a synonym for money in this culture, and the use of it is often measured by its profit potential. If the work makes money, it is time well spent. If the work is not profitable, it is a waste of our time. We have come to define ourselves by what we do to pay the bills. The question "What do you do?" generally means "how do you make your living?" It rarely has anything to do with the calling in one's heart or the time we spend on creative work. In Corita Kent's book, *Learning by Heart*, she writes that in Balinese culture, when you ask a person what he does, he will proudly answer that he is a mask maker or dancer. And if you persist and ask again, "No, I mean how do you get your rice?" he loses interest, his voice drops, and he may turn away, deciding this is a pretty boring conversation. 'Oh that,' he will say."

A friend of mine was raising her children in the early 70s. She was a stay-at-home Mom but felt uncomfortable about not having a "real job" to talk about. When someone asked her at a cocktail party, "What do you do?" she said "I married a rich man. I do anything I want." While the answer was true, it never felt right to her. It was years later that the perfect response came to her, and she called to tell me about it. Now when people ask what she does, she says, *"About what?"*

"Everything I do is in response to something, and I want to be as specific as I can," she said to me, proud and relieved that she had an answer that lived up to who she was.

As creators, we too are responding constantly to the world around us. Every unfolding event is grist for the mill—every human adventure, every relational challenge, every headline. We are stimulated by outside events and we respond creatively, though the seed might take years to come to fruition. The creative process often calls for deep patience, long periods of reflection and incubation. There is no rushing it, anymore than one can naturally rush the birth of a baby. Our creations arrive on their own terms, in their own time.

Having been raised in a culture where time equals money, I was surprised to experience the flip side of that belief when I lived in India for a few months. I was in Gujarat, at a Gandhian ashram. The community was gathering to build a new barn. Close to eighty people met at the edge of a stream, about a quarter of a mile from the building site. Though no one in particular issued any orders, the group formed into a long line from the stream, up a hill, up a ladder against a small cliff, through a meadow and to the site of the new barn, where young women were hauling rocks on their heads for the foundation. It was monsoon season. Though it was early morning the temperature was already 100 degrees and the air was heavy with humidity.

Our job was to pass tin bowls of sand, stones, and water for mortar from the stream to the building site. Hour after hour went by. Not one person complained. Women wrapped in six yards of sari were giggling and gossiping as they passed the bowls. By midmorning, I was soaking wet and losing steam. At one point, I squinted into the wavy heat and scanned the landscape for signs of relief. My eyes landed first on two tractors in a nearby meadow. Then on two idle carts on the side of the road. Moments later, a group of kids passed by leading a team of oxen to the river. It seemed crazy that all this people power was being used when we could just hook up the oxen, the tractor and the carts.

"This is ridiculous!" I shouted to Nayan Bala, an English-speaking woman from Delhi who stood next to me in line. "We've got a ton of people here wasting a whole morning in this heat passing buckets like there's no tomorrow. Why don't we hook up the carts and use them? We could do the job in half the time. Don't you know time is money?"

I knew, even as those final words tumbled out of my mouth, that every one of them was a mistake, but they were traveling too fast to stop. Nayan Bala put her bowl down and walked over to my side. She put her hand on my sweaty arm and whispered in my ear, "These people are proud to be building this barn with their own hands. One day they will bring their children and grandchildren here and tell them how they helped build it, rock by rock. Perhaps you have more to learn about India if you think this is a waste of time."

I was ashamed of myself, ashamed of ever buying into the time-is-money myth and ashamed of criticizing a process that wasn't mine to condemn. It wasn't just India I had more to learn about. It was the whole notion of time, of the time it takes to create, and of how such time can never be wasted. In the process of creating, time is one of the essential ingredients.

When it comes to creating our lives, time is one of the first things we have to manage. A balanced life requires solitude as much as social interaction, silence as much as stimulation. The darkness of the cave is as fertile and essential as the lightness of the commons. We need both to be fulfilled. It's a matter of balancing yin and yang. Wherever there is an imbalance in our lives, there is struggle and pain. If there is balance, there is harmony, in the body and in the body politic.

Your words and sentences can be like gingko to others, just as these sentences may be to you—words that help you remember, that restore your balance, alter your mood, improve your thinking, diminish your depression. As creators ourselves, Ruth and I know the power of the word, the strength of an image, the magic of a metaphor. We are not clad in white coats, but we are clinicians in this laboratory, rethinking formulae, mixing new ingredients, replicating experiments till we learn what works.

We have over 100 years of creative experience, with a handful of masterpieces and a house full of attempts that never quite made it. We dedicate time every day to silence and solitude. I find mine in the comfort of my bed, or my studio, sitting before a candle that connects me to the cosmos. Ruth finds hers on her walks through nature, in the beauty of her rose garden, in her yoga practice. All of our paths are unique and personal, but one thing is common: the time we take *away* from the chaos is a required daily dosage for a creative life.

YOU ARE WORTH THE TIME

I'm perplexed and challenged by the time dilemma, so I decided to work with it, to take it on as an art piece. I took the time (made the time, created the time, used the time) to make a video called *You Are Worth the Time*. I wrote a script, put it to music, used images of people in the process of creating. Then I uploaded it to YouTube.[1] As of today over 58,642 people around the world have watched it. While I finished it years ago, it continues to have a life of its own. Here are the words:

You Are Worth the Time

It's not easy these days making time for our creative work. Voices call us from everywhere demanding our attention, our energy, our time. And many of us, somewhere along the path, got the message that making art was self indulgent so we relegate it to the bottom of our list. It becomes the thing we get to when the laundry is done, the kids asleep, the groceries bought and put away.

We get so caught up in the flurry of our lives that we forget the essential thing about art: that the act of creating is a healing gesture, as sacred as prayer, as essential to our spirit as food to our body. It is our creative work that reveals us to ourselves, allows us to transform our experience and imagination into new forms...forms that sing back to us in a language of symbol who we are, what we are becoming, what it is we have loved and feared.

This is the alchemy of creation: that as my energy fuses with the source of Energy, a newness rises up in the shape of who I am and I myself am altered in the course of its release. I am never the same in the wake of this work. As I create I come into my power, into my wisdom, into that newness which becomes the gift I share with the world.

As a result of the time I spend at my work there is more of me to give, more awareness, more joy, more depth. I become centered in the process, focused on the interior, attuned to the inner voice.

Life is no longer about time and demands and errands. It is about the extraordinary metamorphosis of one thing into another. What begins as cocoon emerges a butterfly, what once was sorrow may now be a song. As I am changed by the art that passes through me in the process of becoming, so am I changed by the creations of others. Having felt the truth of your cobalt blue, my red will remember and its voice will be clearer. In the turn of your phrase, the tenor of your voice, the pulse of your poem, I find fragments of myself I have long forgotten. It is to you I look to find myself, and in your words I find the courage to write my own.

Making time for creative work is like making time for prayer. It is a healing act, a leave taking from the chaos, as we move from the choppy surface toward the stillness of the center. To be an artist it is not necessary to make a living from our creations, nor is it necessary to have work hanging in fine museums, or the praise of critics. It is not necessary that we are published or that famous people own our work. To be an artist it is necessary to live with our eyes wide open, to breathe in the colors of mountain and sky, to know the sound of leaves rustling, the smell of snow, the texture of bark.

It is necessary to rub our hands all over life, to sing when and where we want, to take in every detail and to jump when we get to the edge of the cliff. To be an artist is to notice every beautiful and tragic thing, to cry freely, to collect experience and shape it into forms that others can use.

It is not to whine about not having time but to be creative with every moment. To be an artist is not to wait for others to define us but to define ourselves, to claim our lives.

Our cities and towns are full of poets, playwrights, composers and painters who drive buses, work in offices, wait on tables to pay the rent. Few of us are paid much for our creative work so we squeeze it in to the hours we have left after working other jobs. We write our novels in the wee hours of the morning, work in our darkrooms through the night, write poetry on subway cars, finish essays in waiting rooms and parking lots. We rarely think of ourselves as artists, though it is our creative work that brings us to life, feeds our spirits and sees us through the dark. We may feel alone, but we are not alone, there are hundreds, thousands in the night, doing as we do, trading this sacred time for the bliss of creating.

There are a lot of things we don't have in life but time is not one of them. Time is all we have, one lifetime, under this name, to produce a body of work that says, "This is how I saw the world." Your work is worthy of whatever time it takes.

THE REACH OF OUR WORK

Aside from YouTube statistics, there are few ways for any of us to measure the reach of our work, to know its impact in any concrete way, but that should not stop us from creating and sharing it as near and far as we can. All you have to do is think about the difference music makes in your life, reflect on a few movies that have brought you to tears, remember the feeling of being in a crowded theater watching a play or shouting out "Bravo!" during a standing ovation. Nothing has the power that the arts have to break open our hearts and melt the frozenness within.

This is why when we want to take a stand, make a difference, we turn to the arts. The arts go right to the heart of the receiver just as they come from the heart of the sender. Their frequency is higher than the roar of the crowds. Creative works reconnect the brain and heart, open the channels where vital energies come alive. Our creations heal us as they come to life, and often heal others in ways unknown to us. Taking the time to create is an act of generosity, an act of courage and faith.

High school students around the country are using video and YouTube as a way to contribute to a brighter world. One visit to youthactivismproject.org is all it will take to renew your faith in today's youth. In every social arena, there are young teens involved in projects that are raising the consciousness of the American public, calling for corporations to be environmentally accountable, drawing attention to issues that affect us all. They often create entertaining and informative videos that not only inform the community about a social problem, but inspire other youth to become engaged as well.

Here are a few examples from the website. You can view the videos online.[2] At age 15, Kelsey Juilana became one of the plaintiffs in a lawsuit demanding the State of Oregon reduce carbon emissions and climate warming. She says "we have a lot of corruption and money that influences our legislators" and this legal strategy now has moved to the U.S. Supreme Court. To learn more about the Public Trust Doctrine: http://www.ourchildrenstrust.org/youth-engagement

- Earth Guardians continue to organize support to ban fracking in Colorado using many strategies including art activism, demonstrating and testifying before key decision makers. Outspoken Xiuhtezcatl Martinez, 13, gave an emotional and information packed presentation the Boulder County Commission.
- HS football player Dahkota Kicking Bear Brown started NERDS which stands for Native Education Raising Dedicated Students. In addition to a peer to peer support group, this 15-year-old recently called on Congress to demand an end to school and professional team and mascot names like the Washington Redskins
- Pelican Island Elementary School students in Florida made dozens of presentations to the School Board, the Indian River County Commission, their U.S. Representative, and the Secretary of the U.S. Interior Department to protect the habitat of the scrub jay, an endangered species. Ultimately, the Eco-Troop received a matching grant of more than $200,000 from the U.S. Fish & Wildlife Service to purchase undeveloped lots from private landowners for this wildlife sanctuary.
- The Beachwood High School Ecology Club's investigation of the curbside recycling programs concluded that none of the 4,872 tons of residential trash in their Cleveland suburb was actually recycled. The findings were first disclosed in the school newspaper by Stephanie Bleyer, 16, who wrote, "Ladies and gentlemen of the city government, in the future when you sign an ambiguous contract [with Global Waste, Inc.] and advertise false city programs, give the whole true story or else student journalists like myself will." This evidence caused the mayor and others responsible to overhaul the city's solid waste reduction program.

Research among Millennials (born 1980 and later) shows them being highly-connected through technology and social media, but they are not just tweeting, retweeting and tagging photos. They are using their networks to share information about social issues and advocate for a wide variety of causes. In a USA Today article on Millennials and activism, Benjamin Kennedy, a University of Vermont student said:

Repeated exposure to a cause on social media may not change someone's actions, but I think it has the power to spark a change in their thoughts. Social media has a way of "humanizing" causes and helping people to realize that everyone has been impacted/ knows someone who has been impacted by the issues of, for example, racism, queer rights, mental illness or chronic physical illness in some way.[3]

While we hear little of Millennial activism through our standard media outlets, it is well documented that this generation of adults is committing its time and energy to a world that works for everyone. To live imaginative and inspired lives doesn't take genius, money, or luck. It takes time, the courage to go within, and commitment. It takes verve and stamina and rebellious originality to keep on imagining, creating, speaking out, showing up.

In order to give voice to our authentic thought instead of inherited beliefs, we need time to sort out one from the other. We have to listen to our own words and assess them for realness. We have to weigh our remarks against our lived experience. Are we speaking what we have learned *from our own lives*? That is the work of evolutionary creators, of creatives who are aware and alert that with these very words we give shape to our reality. The word *is* made flesh, over and over and over again. As we think and speak, so it becomes.

We cannot keep repeating stale platitudes. We must look to see what ordeals we have mastered and share the story of the steps we took. We must give heart to each other. Share our clues and what we learned along the way. As a people, we are letting go of thought patterns that have dominated and diminished us for years, or "remounting the slope of thought," as philosopher Henri Bergson puts. The old is dissipating and the new is being born, ushered in by those of us who are not afraid of being different.

Robert Grudin in *The Grace of Great Things,* reminds us: "Creativity is dangerous. We cannot open ourselves to new insight without endangering the security of our prior assumptions. We cannot propose new ideas without risking disapproval and rejection. Creative achievement is the boldest initiative of mind, an adventure that takes its hero simultaneously to the rim of knowledge and the limits of propriety. Its pleasure is not the comfort of the safe harbor, but the thrill of the reaching sail."[4]

Evolutionary creators *become* visionary leaders by letting go of the security of prior assumptions. It is the only pathway out of conditioned thought patterns that limit us immensely and lead to more chaos than coherence. Conscious creators are bridge-builders who connect the local and the global, the past and the future, the heart and the brain. They know the power of emotion and they use it courageously. They see themselves as a whole that is a part of a larger whole—and it is to this larger whole that they dedicate their lives. And if one wonders where meaning comes from, where joy and passion and purpose come from, it is from this gesture of service to the whole.

STRIVING TO EFFECT CHANGE BY EXAMPLE

When the Beatles came on the scene, they brought a whole new sound that rocked the world. When Braque, Cezanne and Picasso introduced cubism to the world, they revolutionized European painting and sculpture and inspired new movements in music, literature and architecture. When Gandhi introduced the practice of Satyagraha or non-violent resistance, the philosophy inspired Dr. Martin Luther King, Jr. and future movements for civil rights, peace and global justice.

When I was in Manila in the 1980s, I witnessed and photographed the people's revolution. It was peaceful, and successful, and they ousted the dictator that had kept them impoverished. Thousands of individuals poured into the city everyday, carrying signs that identified their work: farmers, factory workers, fishermen, domestic workers. They had taken the injustice long enough and they were committed to a peaceful change in the power structure. They didn't know or care how long it would take. They marched, they handed out flyers, they glued WANTED: MARCOS posters everywhere. And Filipino musicians came from everywhere to sing to them all night long. They all stood on the shoulders of Mahatma Gandhi. They knew they could do it because it had been done before. This is how we move each other.

Each of us as creator is contributing to the fabric of the cultures we inhabit. What we do or fail to do is consequential. A hundred years from now, if your descendants did a search to see what you stood for, they would reach their conclusions from the tracks you are making. If there are none, it will say one thing. If there is evidence from your life—stories handed down, letters written, photographs taken, organizations started—these things will be the legacy for who you are.

The world provides us with contexts for our creations and the back-drops for our lives. It provides the dramatic elements, the locations, the conflicts, and the characters. You are the hero on a quest for something. What *is* that thing and what battles are you engaged in to find what you are seeking? These things are our raw materials. Your palette is made of sky blue, red bricks, green trees, gray cement. The year is now. The location is here. "One must have a vision to build towards, and that vision must spring from the nature of the world we live in," writes novelist Doris Lessing,

This is it. This is your studio, your classroom, your temple, and every event is a scene in the play of your life. You are the writer, the director, the actor, and the acted upon. There is an incredible story unfolding and it's all yours. Do you know what it is? Are you making something of it?

"The end of art is peace," says poet Seamus Heaney, the Nobel Laureate from Ireland. "I can't think of a case where poems changed the world, but what they do is change people's understanding of what's going on in the world." That's the gift of creativity. It's the metaphor that carries us over into a broader understanding of our own world and our own experience. In his Nobel acceptance speech, Heaney speaks of several poets and their impact:

> In one of the poems best known to students in my generation, a poem which could be said to have taken the nutrients of the symbolist movement and made them available in capsule form, the American poet Archibald MacLeish affirmed that "A poem should be equal to/not true." As a defiant statement of poetry's gift for telling truth but telling it slant, this is both cogent and corrective. Yet there are times when a deeper need enters, when we want the poem to be not only pleasurably right but compellingly wise, not only a surprising variation played upon the world, but a re-tuning of the world itself. We want the surprise to be transitive like the impatient thump which unexpectedly restores the picture to the television set, or the electric shock which sets the fibrillating heart back to its proper rhythm. We want what the woman wanted in the prison queue in Leningrad, standing there blue with cold and whispering for fear, enduring the terror of Stalin's regime and asking the poet Anna Akhmatova if she could describe it all, if her art could be equal to it.[5]

Anna Akhmatova was a Russian poet who spoke the truth during the Stalinist years. There was an unofficial ban on Akhmatova's poetry from 1925 until 1940. Her husband Nikolai Gumilev was executed in 1921 by the Bolsheviks, and she remarried Nikolai Punin who died in a Siberian labor camp in 1953. Akhmatova devoted herself to literary criticism and translations. During the latter part of the 1930s, she composed a long poem, Requiem, dedicated to the memory of Stalin's victims.

Following World War II, there was an official decree banning publication of her poetry and Andrey Zhadanov, the Secretary of the Central Committee, expelled her from the Writer's Union, calling her "half nun, half harlot." She began writing and publishing again in 1958, but her work was often censored. Young poets like Joseph Brodsky were drawn to her, for she represented a link with the pre-Revolutionary past that had been destroyed by the Communists.

Though the official government opposed her work during her lifetime, she was deeply loved by the Russian people, in part because she remained there and kept writing. Many of her works are reactions to the horror of the Stalinist Terror, during which time she endured artistic repression as well as tremendous personal loss.

The event that Seamus Heaney was referring to is written here in her own words. The Yezhovschina she mentions was a campaign of political repression in the Soviet Union orchestrated by Joseph Stalin from 1934 to 1939. This is how Anna Akhmatova told the story:

In the awful days of the Yezhovschina I passed seventeen months in the outer waiting line of the prison visitors in Leningrad. Once, somebody 'identified' me there. Then a woman, standing behind me in the line, who, of course, never heard my name, waked up from the torpor, typical for us all there, and asked me, whispering into my ear (all spoke only in a whisper there):

"And can you describe this?"

And I answered:

"Yes, I can."

Then the weak similarity of a smile glided over that, what had once been her face.

April 1, 1957; Leningrad [6]

The woman asked the poet if she could use her gift to tell the world what was going on. "Can you describe this?" And of course, Anna Akhmatova dedicated her life to describing those events, so that history could be a lesson to the future and not repeated.

Our task is not so daunting, perhaps, but it is equally compelling: to tell the story of what is happening, to share our perspective, to offer our ideas. Otherwise history may compare us to those German civilians who witnessed the trains, smelled the smoke, heard the gunfire, but who say all along they never knew what was going on.

We know what is happening. We have information reaching us minute by minute of our impact on the planet, on other countries, on each other. We know the rainforests are being decimated. We know our food and water is being compromised. We know our oceans are filling with plastics, our icecaps are melting. We know which corporations are most to blame. We know we could easily feed every person on the planet if we changed our priorities. Each of us is a part of history being made. Each of us is an actor in the global play, no matter how local or limited our scope. This is an invitation to rethink your role.

While we were working on this chapter, Ruth had an experience that she reflects on here:

When we started the chapter on time, I started thinking about my old Pilates group. We came together for two to three days a week at our Pilates studio, walked in, greeted each other and began our workout. Over the eight or ten years we worked out together, we became a close-knit group. We showed up even if we were tired because we didn't want to miss anything. We were intertwined in each other's lives. We talked every day we were together about our families, raising children, which colleges to visit. We especially chuckled about the things our spouses or significant others were up to. We gave each other presents at Christmas or Hanukah, cards on our birthdays and continually talked about getting together for a girl's night at someone's home just for laughs, some great food and some light libations.

Every time we brought our calendars into our session, we never could agree on a date because our time was so limited. Time slipped away and then we began to drift apart. Life got in the way. I think I was the first to leave because I had to have knee surgery and decided not to return thinking that Pilates might have been the culprit.

In those short years since we grew apart, one woman lost her husband to cancer after a long illness. Another's husband committed suicide on Thanksgiving. One had a brain tumor and malignant melanoma, and another just passed away from cancer as I write this.

I am so saddened that we didn't make the time to get together and enjoy each other. Then, we didn't know that many of us didn't have much time left. I am sure if we had known what lay ahead, we would have cleared our calendars, penciled in dates, joyously made our pot luck food and come together for laughs and friendship and most of all, memories.

You have your whole life in your hands. You are writing your part every day with every choice you make. The more peaceful you are, the better your life. The calmer you are, the wiser your choices. The more mindful you are, the more brilliant your creations. And all of this starts with time for yourself. Time all alone. Twenty minutes a day could make a huge difference. Twenty minutes could open a portal to wonder. Twenty minutes could be that threshold to paradise, the pathway to bliss. It could be the very thing your soul is seeking.

CHAPTER 5

———— ⌣ ————

THE TRIPLE BOTTOM LINE: WHY BUSINESS NEEDS CREATIVITY TO SUCCEED

*Freedom is actually a bigger game than power. Power is
about what you can control. Freedom is about what you
can unleash.*

HARRIET RUBIN

SCOUTING FOR ORIGINAL THINKERS

I WALKED INTO one of the largest corporate offices in Des Moines, Iowa.
The front lobby was as huge as any hotel lobby I had been in, and their
mission statement was engraved in the granite wall that towered above
me. They were promising to "maintain the highest standards of integrity
and professionalism with their client." Pretty dull, I thought, as I looked
around for a smiling face.

I had come to speak with their staff on Original Thinking and
Innovation. I was invited as the author of the book *The Art of Original
Thinking: The Making of a Thought Leader*, which Ruth proposed and
funded as part of her campaign to launch more women thought leaders onto the national stage. It was in 2006, a few years after Ruth and
I had become friends and colleagues. Ruth identified me as a leader,
respected my creativity, and invited me to write a business book on
visionary leadership that had some creative verve. Nationally, it won
three book awards and led to several speaking engagements. The one in
Des Moines was one of them.

As I set up my laptop, employees filed into the auditorium through several doorways and took their seats. There were about two hundred people in the room. No one spoke to each other or looked around. No one smiled. I had a PowerPoint presentation of twelve *New Yorker* cartoons addressing workplace issues, boss–employee conflicts, and paradigm shifts in corporate America. I used them for my talking points. My plan was to get people laughing, provoke new ideas, share some inspiring stories about companies who were "doing well by doing good," ask a few engaging questions, and create a conversation of consequence that would leave them inspired and enlivened.

I showed the first three cartoons and silence reverberated throughout the room. I wondered why; every other audience from California to New York found them hilarious. Not this crowd. When the fourth cartoon failed to generate a response, I turned up the lights and moved to the center of the stage. "Look, these cartoons are really funny," I said. "They're hysterical. I'm giving you permission to laugh. We're here to have a good time. Come on...," I urged.

I heard someone mumble something about having to be there. Another voice from the other side said something about being paid to be there. It was deadly. In all my years of speaking, I've grown accustomed to people responding positively and emotionally to my down-home style and invitation to show up and be part of the magic. But not here. Not at this Fortune 500 company with 13,500 global employees and their big commitment to integrity. It was as if they had taken out their hearts for the day and just brought their brains to work.

Both Ruth and I have spoken to business audiences across the country and have found this a common experience. Ruth said once, upon coming back from such an occasion,

It's like they don't know the value of their own diversity. They have people from all over, with an extraordinary range of experience and insight, but they don't know how to capitalize on this. They don't know how to foster a creative culture. Their people aren't encouraged to have fun or build camaraderie with each other. That's the tragedy.

Contrast this with David Kelley's company IDEO, a global design firm in Silicon Valley. As a young designer, Kelley wrote a letter to a friend that included these words: "I want to start a company with all my best friends as employees."[1] Building on this, IDEO today is made up of more than five hundred people in offices around the world. The web page describing life at IDEO announces, "Together, we navigate each day with curiosity, optimism, and a sense of humor. We are makers, designers, hackers, builders, thinkers, explorers, writers, listeners, risk-takers, and doers—and we love what we do."[2] Now there's a statement worth chiseling.

David Kelley, the company's founder and chair, has posted a short video on the website called "Stop Talking and Start Making."[3] It's whimsical, profound, luminous. It's about the value of bringing your creative ideas to the table and putting yourself out there—as Nike might put it *Just Do It.* IDEO created many icons of the digital generation—the first mouse for Apple, the first Palm Treo smartphone, the thumbs up/thumbs down button on Tivo's remote control. But what excites them is unlocking the creative potential of people and organizations so they can innovate routinely. IDEO's motto is not etched into a granite wall, but it is posted for all to see. "*We help organizations build creative culture and the internal systems required to sustain innovation and launch new ventures.*"[4] They know the necessity of creative culture, of having an environment that fuels originality and relationship.

Tim Brown, current president and CEO of IDEO, says, "Design thinking is a human-centered approach to innovation that draws from the designer's toolkit to integrate the needs of people, the possibilities of technology, and the requirements for business success."[5] The IDEO community believes that innovation happens through networks of inspired people, and they have created a nonprofit wing called IDEO. org that allows them to collaborate at scale and effect change faster and more systemically because of the networks they are creating. The nonprofit was launched as a philanthropic outlet for IDEO employees and includes a fellowship program for outside talent that brings future leaders from the worlds of design and social enterprise to join forces. Included in the network are NGOs, foundations, nonprofits, government entities, public health groups, and people affiliated with academic institutions such as Stanford University and the Royal College of Art.

Jocelyn Wyatt and Patrice Martin are the co-leads and executive directors of IDEO.org. Their mission is twofold: To apply human-centered design to poverty-related challenges, and in the process, to change the way that for-profit businesses can use their resources to create social good. Although they have accomplished tremendous gains in several countries as well as the United States, IDEO.org is not slowing down. In a recent *Fast Company* article, the IDEO.org team shares their vision of influencing the way the entire design and social sectors view their role as global citizens.[6]

One strategy for spreading their ideas of human-centered design is to share their resources. They have produced the *Human Centered Design Toolkit*, a free guide for NGOs and social enterprises that's been downloaded more than a hundred thousand times. They also teamed with Acumen to develop a seven-week online course in Human Centered Design for Social Innovation. These are both easy to access online.

IDEO.org also collaborates with Moneythink, a Chicago-based organization, which facilitates financial literacy in youth. Moneythink sees a vision of the world in which youth, regardless of background, can enter adulthood equipped with the confidence, habits, and tools to navigate the financial challenges of the real world. The program trains college students to become mentors and deliver financial curriculum in high schools. Their 600 mentors have in turn trained 4,500 students in 84 classrooms nationwide.

Moneythink came to IDEO.org to explore the opportunity for mobile tools that would expand their curriculum outside of the classroom. After exploring the financial-decision-making mindset of high school students, the IDEO.org team created an app that allows students to engage in challenges and get real time feedback from their peers and mentors about their financial decisions. In his online update about the Moneythink collaboration, designer and social entrepreneur Rafael Smith writes,

> The primary focus of the Moneythink mobile app project is to improve the financial decision-making of college-bound 11th and 12th grade students. Students in this age group face unique first-time financial choices – managing incomes from part-time jobs and government funds, signing up for a bank accounts, utilizing credit and debit cards, and applying for student loans. We've learned during our research that young people ages 18-25 are the fastest growing segment for bankruptcy in the US. And youth are not alone. Half of all Americans are living from paycheck to paycheck and have household savings of less than $1,200.[7]

The vital and innovative companies of today are uncovering creative energies through a variety of strategies. Systems-thinking expert Peter Senge writes,

> Learning organizations are those organizations where people continually expand their capacity to create the results they truly desire, where new and expansive patterns of thinking are nurtured, where collective aspiration is set free, and where people are continually learning to see the whole together. [8]

Yes, but *how* does a company nurture expansive patterns of thinking? *How* does a company encourage individuals to *see the whole together*, which is, in a nutshell, the purpose of systems thinking? A tweet delivered a great line by Lisa Boddell of futurethink in a lecture on performance: "If you want a better approach to change, change the approach."

At the Social Ventures Network (SVN) 2014 spring conference, I listened to Walter Robb, co-CEO of Whole Foods, acknowledge that their success is dependent upon the collective energy and intelligence of all of their team members. They are committed to policies that address the needs and imaginations of the employees. About 93 percent of stock options awarded since their IPO have gone to workers. Executive pay is limited to nineteen times the average frontline employee.[9] To put that in perspective, the CEO-to-worker pay gaps published by *Christian Science Monitor* are as follows:

1196:1 for McDonald's
1096:1 for Starbucks
1007:1 for Dollar General
924:1 for T.J. Maxx
824:1 for Target
779:1 for Wal-Mart
769:1 for CVS Caremark
666:1 for Best Buy
558:1 for AT&T.

With the 19:1 ratio at Whole Foods, and an average fifteen dollars per hour salary, they are ensuring employees feel valued for their work. They also qualify for stock options, profit sharing, health insurance, and paid time off for volunteer work. To keep the working environment transparent, financial data is released to employees so they can see how the company is doing and become more informed stakeholders and stockholders.

In an interview for *What Is Enlightenment* magazine, Robb said,

We're not retailers who have a mission—we're missionaries who retail. At the very heart and soul of Whole Foods is the mission. We're here to make a real difference in people's health and well-being, in the health and well-being of the planet, and in creating a workplace based on love and respect. So we put our customers and Team Members before our shareholders. And if you compare our performance to other publicly traded food companies, it's superior. A thousand bucks invested in Whole Foods at the beginning in 1992 would be worth well over thirty thousand now."[10]

Whole Foods is the largest organic and natural foods grocer in the United States. It has beaten Wal-Mart in overall and comparable store sales growth, while profoundly impacting how Americans eat. A group of sixty employees, known as Team Members, drafted a Declaration of Interdependence that sits on their website and helps to explain their phenomenal success. They have created an Animal Compassion Foundation to provide education and research services to ranchers and meat producers around the world who want to remain economically viable while maintaining standards of excellence for animal welfare. To do this, they are partnering with animal welfare advocacy groups and the farmers and ranchers they do business with.

They have also established a Whole Planet Foundation, which is partnering with EARTH University in Costa Rica, Universidad Francisco Marroquin in Guatemala, and Grameen Trust of Bangladesh to conduct a micro-loan program to help women in these areas develop their own micro-enterprises. Whole Foods is concentrating its efforts in the regions where it purchases pineapples, bananas, and coffee, and their goal is to assist up to 8,500 women in their efforts to become self-supporting entrepreneurs. They support the projects through the global Five-Percent Day, allocating five percent of all global sales on a designated day to microcredit loans.

Shopping at Whole Foods is usually an immersion in diversity. The workers are as colorful as their organic vegetables, representing a vast array of cultures and lifestyles. Though they don't mention diversity as a company commitment, research is showing the benefits of doing so. In his book *The Wisdom of Crowds*, James Surowiecki cites the work of Scott Page, a political scientist at the University of Michigan, whose experiments with computer-simulated problem solving agents revealed some interesting findings on the subject. Page set up groups of ten to twenty agents, each endowed with a different set of skills, and had them solve a sophisticated problem. Individually, some did well at solving the problem and some were less effective.

What Page found was that "a group made up of some smart agents and some not-so-smart agents almost always did better than a group made up just of smart agents.... Adding in a few people who *know less, but have different skills,* actually improves the group's performance."[11] Bringing diverse members into the group, even if they are less experienced or capable, actually increases the group's wisdom because what the new members do know is not redundant with what everyone else knows. Any board of directors, business or nonprofit, that is striving to expand its creativity need only look into its own diversity and ensure ample differences in its cultural makeup.

Ruth has worked as marketing director for three high tech start-up companies and has served on the boards of several national nonprofit organizations. She has worked in diverse and non-diverse situations. She has participated in groups that were extremely creative and groups that didn't take a creative approach. What she has observed, in terms of differences, provides interesting empirical evidence on the subject of creativity in business.

> The companies I worked with all had innovative products and might have been successful, but they did not comprehend the value of systems thinking. They had their creative thinkers, usually engineers or physicists. And they all had staff in Research and Development, Purchasing, Manufacturing, Inventory and Quality Control, Sales, and my department, Marketing. Every meeting I ever attended in all three companies went the same. Each department gave their reports and talked about what the competition was doing. Then they scheduled the next meeting, and everyone went back to their cubicles. As if they were all in

separate silos, with their own objectives and missions, there was a lack of cross-pollination between departments or discussion about the organization as a single system.

We never discussed our own process, never analyzed the culture we were creating or the outcome. Diversity, creativity, community—these topics just didn't come up. It was an isolated and isolating experience, and on some level, I'm sure that's what contributed to the failures of these startups.

Diversity gives you a richer outcome. Malcolm Forbes says, "Diversity is the art of thinking independently together."[12] Jennifer Fonstad, co-founder of Aspect Ventures, tells the story of an all-male development team that built an app for finding babysitters but inadvertently designed it so that it was almost unusable for women with long fingernails.[13] That might not have happened with a more diverse team.

Adam Quinton of Lucas Point Ventures looks for diversity in the teams he invests in, trusting women-led projects will have an edge over standard VCs. "When people ask why I invest in diverse teams, I tell them it's because I'm going to make more money. If investing in diverse teams improves the probability of success and lowers the risk of failure, why wouldn't I?" he asks. Quinton has backed eight companies over the past two years, all with female CEOs.[14] Any visionary who is looking to put together a group of powerhouse creative thinkers knows by now that the best move is to create a team of people with the most wide-ranging experience. That means women, people of color, people from other cultures and religious groups, people with disabilities, people from a variety of classes. What will happen is anything but predictable. The only sure thing is that creative ideas will be flying around like confetti at a victory parade.

It takes many minds coming together to discover the solution that is already dwelling in our midst. This might be one reason the IDEO model of bringing many different types of brains and thinking to each project has worked so well. They have gone from being a product-oriented company with unique concepts, such as a new nail polish experience, redesigning school food and cafeterias, and looking at a new approach to aging. In most of their brainstorming, they are creating "experiences" not products.

This is what Lisa Boddell was talking about when she mentioned the phrase "change the approach." It's a mindset change, like the difference between asking "How can we be the best company in the world?" and "How can we be the best company *for* the world?" The questions we ask have the potential to get people excited and engaged. If a company asks questions that tap people's imaginations for original solutions, it will find the stratospheric innovation it's looking for.

The challenge has more to do with creativity than anything else. For loyalty, happiness, diligence, and dedication to occur in the workplace, the creators of that workplace need to keep stoking the imaginations of every worker there. From the CEO to the receptionist, the engineers to the marketing department, the diversity of the whole is what needs to be mined. As Max DePree said, "The measure of leadership is not the quality of the head, but the tone of the body."[15] There are no pat formulas to rely on to motivate people. The new ABCs of leadership are

Authenticity
Balance
Consciousness

The new workforce is not nearly as excited about bottom-line decision-making as it is about triple-bottom line thinking, which means giving equal consideration to people, planet, and profits. According to a survey on green employment conducted by MonsterTRAK.com, an employment Web site targeted at students and entry-level hires, 80 percent of young professionals are interested in securing a job that has a positive impact on the environment, and 92 percent would be more inclined to work for a company that is environmentally friendly.[16]

Lindsey Pollak, millennial workplace expert and author of *Getting from College to Career*, says millennials—those born after 1982—now account for about 25 percent of the U.S. population. "There are 76 million of them. Millennials have grown up in a different world than Baby Boomers—those born between 1946 and 1964. Thanks to the Internet, they are used to getting information fast and they have a great awareness of what is going on in the world. They believe it is their duty to do something about the environment," says Polak.[17] With this rapidly changing, increasingly-demanding workforce, how can businesses reinvent themselves as relevant, conscious and attractive workplaces?

AHEAD OF THE CURVE

Adaptation to changes in a culture of any kind—corporate, national, institutional—happens with a certain amount of predictability. There are always the risk takers, the early adopters, the slow-to-believe, the resisters. The Rogers bell curve is a visual illustration of how this plays out.

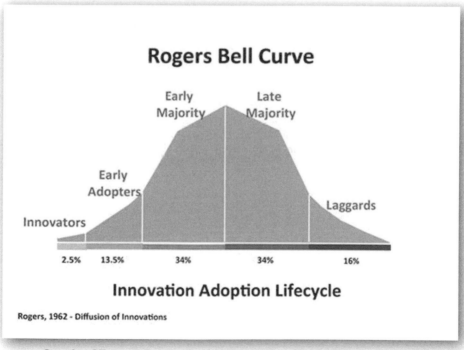

Graph of Everett Rogers Technology Adoption Lifecycle model.[18]

Less than 2.5 percent of the population has the ideas and courage to begin large, systemic changes. Do the other 97.5 percent of people follow innovation and adopt new change philosophies? No. In fact, innovation and new ideas, cornerstones of creativity, are always a hard sell in the beginning. It is the Late Adopters and the Laggards that come around last, when everyone else has seen the light but them. The Innovators and Early Adopters understand that they need new models and new tools, such as the models that distinguish the IDEOs of the world from the three failed startups that Ruth worked for.

In his book *A Whole New Mind: Why Right Brainers Will Rule the Future*, Daniel H. Pink writes that current global conditions such as abundance, Asian outsourcing, and automation, are setting the stage for a shift from the Information Age to the Conceptual Age. In the Conceptual Age, creative thinking skills will be the key. Every institution in the country is weighed down by its own history, by old traditions and outmoded prac-tices. The Great Rethinking that is occurring right now is happening everywhere, and the question is pretty much the same: How do we cause transformation in our own culture that will lead to energized and cre-ative employees, well-served customers, environmentally sound policies, and improved bottom lines? People, planet, profits.

This is not an issue to be solved by leaders, but to be explored by everyone who is involved in the organizational culture. It is a family issue worthy of family pondering. The solutions will surface from the commu-nity-at-large once the members feel authentically asked and engaged. Businesses are undergoing massive overhauls to meet the requirements of this moment in history. So are schools, information systems, govern-ments, you name it.

Melissa Peirce, senior managing partner at The Wellspring Group, which specializes in national technology staffing, says that many of the companies they work for are asking entirely different questions than they might have asked a decade ago, questions such as "What makes some-one successful in our environment?" Their interviewing strategies now include behavioral inquiries as they look for emotional capacities that are right for their cultures. "Larger companies have plans in place to allow for employee volunteer work or sabbaticals for foreign travel. They are becoming more socially-conscious, hiring for attitude more than skillset," says Peirce, who has been watching the trends over twenty years. "When we started our business, colleges were not offering so many sophisticated computer degrees, so companies were looking for employees with arts degrees. They were seeking creative thinkers and problems solvers."[18]

An article on leadership in a recent *Fast Company* magazine was titled, "Is an MFA the New MBA?" It reported on an IBM global study of more than 1,500 CEOs from 60 countries and 33 industries which found that the most important skill for navigating our increasingly complex, volatile, and uncertain world is none other than *creativity*. The consensus of the CEOs is that creative leaders

- expect to make more business model changes to realize their strategies;
- invite disruptive innovation, encourage others to drop outdated approaches and take balanced risks;
- consider previously unheard-of ways to drastically change the enterprise for the better;
- are comfortable with ambiguity and experiment to create new business models;
- score much higher on innovation as a crucial capability;
- are courageous and visionary enough to alter the status quo; and
- will invent new models based on entirely different assumptions.[19]

Once thought to be at the opposite ends of the personality scale, the soft world of artistry and the hard world of business are learning the value of working together. MBA programs around the world are embracing arts-based learning to develop leadership qualities such as insight, creativity, teamwork, and social responsibility in their students.

Ruth's experience as an artist, a philanthropist, and an advocate for creative problem solving, has helped her connect the dots between sharp business acumen and creative, responsible innovation. She writes:

Because of my philanthropic work over the years, and my choice to work in a collaborative fashion with other groups, I have developed skills as a connector and a convener. I connect people to causes and to other people who can move the needle. I bring diverse people together and provide a safe and non-threatening atmosphere to stretch their imaginations. After many years of practice, I have developed a toolkit that helps groups achieve their goals. My singular agenda is to move the mission forward.

I did not get a degree to learn these skills. I listened. I inquired. I watched how groups worked together, taking note of their successes and their failures. And I contributed from my own experience whenever I could. My experience helps me intuitively understand the value of diversity, not because I learned of it in the latest business book, but because I've played the role of the marginal one, the token woman, the token artist. It's not clear to everyone at the outset why I'm there, but by the end, my value is apparent.

I was invited to participate in a four-day brainstorming session on the East Coast to look at the way medical care was currently delivered in this country and how we might shift to a more patient-centered approach with an emphasis on health creation and prevention. The folks asked to participate were an esteemed group of medical people, a couple former governors, high-ranking medical military officers, project managers, and me.

When it was time to introduce myself, I stated that I'm an artist and am in the extraordinary position of being a philanthropist with a focus on integrative medicine. I also explained that I've been doing what I do for a long time. Perhaps you can imagine what this group was thinking about me, and I would have thought the same thing myself. What tools and capabilities does an artist, philanthropist, integrative medicine specialist have that justify being part of this learned and accomplished group of academics and military brass?

We began our discussions, and where it felt right, I contributed. At the end of three days, the group was listening intently when I spoke. They felt I had a unique perspective that was helpful. As we were going to our rooms after dinner one evening, one of the military officers said, "I keep trying to figure out how you think and process complex issues the way you do. I understand you are an artist. I am not seeing it." That night I had an epiphany on a topic I've thought long and hard about.

I think the way I do because I am a creative thinker and an artist. I am a problem solver every time I paint.

Painting or creating is a very complex business and requires working your way through a process in your mind in order to believe it will work on canvas. Sometimes I work from the bottom up, analyzing each process as it unfolds—other times I work from the top down—visualizing the finished product and working backwards to see what processes are required for a completed piece.

So every time I pick up a *Wall Street Journal* or some other periodical, I'm not surprised to find an article on why a creative/artist should be at every table helping to create better products and solve business dilemmas. Seems like I was ahead of the curve, but I am not the only one. One of my favorite poets, David Whyte, writes "A good artist, it is often said, is fifty to one hundred years ahead of their time. An artist must depict this new world before all the evidence is in. To wait for all the evidence to be in is to recognize it through a competitor's product."[20]

I have met David Whyte a few times in different contexts, once as the keynote speaker at a medical conference in Calgary. He has a charismatic and commanding presence. His voice reflects the lilting Irish brogue of his Irish maternal ancestry, even though he was brought up in Yorkshire, England. He is a true Irish poet and his concentration has been in lifting up humanity. He found his niche by bringing his poetry to corporate America. His diverse current and past clients include companies like The Boeing Company, Astra-Zenica, and Harvard Medical School. The list is extensive.

So why would Big Business bring an Irish poet into their companies? What does he do for them that keeps them asking him back? The language of poets Dante, Eliot, and Blake, as well as Whyte's own poetry, resonate with humanity, including businesspeople and CEOs. Many of these executives and managers are not able to bring their best selves to work each day. They suffer a disconnect between who they are at home, with family, and who they are expected to be on the job. What if corporate culture doesn't bridge the many worlds we inhabit?

Some executives find it hard to explain what David Whyte does, but most acknowledge he is a storyteller and a poet. He causes people to think. Even at first, if you are taken aback as to why a poet is gracing your strategic planning meeting, after listening to him, you'll begin to understand. Take this poem, for instance, where his description of how poetry comes to him is not unlike the description one might offer about a great insight, epiphany, or idea.

The Lightest Touch

Good poetry begins with
the lightest touch,
a breeze arriving from nowhere,
a whispered healing arrival,
a word in your ear,
a settling into things,
then like a hand in the dark
it arrests your whole body
steeling you for revelation.

In the silence that follows
a great line

you can feel Lazarus
deep inside
even the laziest, most deathly afraid
part of you,
lift up his hands and walk toward the light.[21]

When he speaks to companies, he recites dozens of stories and poems to help bring to life the experience and emotion of change. David says such poems help managers and other employees to rethink their daily habits and assumptions, thus stirring up some creative juices. His work enters into the brain and then filters down to the heart space where the feelings and emotions for change occur.

IT'S ABOUT ENGAGEMENT

Corporate America is not only listening to David Whyte, a poet, but to another creative person, author Brené Brown, as well. Brown is an American scholar, author of *Daring Greatly* and *Gifts of Imperfection*. She is a professor at the University of Houston who explores the subjects of shame and vulnerability.

Ruth had the pleasure of spending time with Brown at the University of Minnesota's Conference for Spirituality and Healing in 2013, and during the course of their conversation, she told the story of how she came to write on something that folks were uncomfortable speaking about. After talking with a thousand people as part of her research project to identify what makes people feel inadequate, Brown understood the role that comparisons play in our feelings of self-worth. She found that we're much more willing to take risks and be creative when our self-worth isn't on the line. Letting go of comparison is a prerequisite for creativity.

Since her TED Talk at TEDx Houston in June 2010, which caught the attention of CEOs, managers, and decision makers in business, her talk has been subtitled in forty-eight languages and has had more than sixteen million viewers. She hit a chord with people who run some of the biggest companies in our country and has become a sought after speaker in many corporate venues. Brown writes in *The Gifts of Imperfection*,

> I define connection as the energy that exists between people when they feel seen, heard, and valued; when they can give and receive without judgment; and when they derive sustenance and strength from the relationship. And, authenticity is a collection of choices that we have to make every day. It's about the choice to show up and be real. The choice to be honest. The choice to let our true selves be seen.[22]

Both David Whyte and Brené Brown talk about relationship, risk, vulnerability—the same things that businesses are dealing with in the quest to get right for these times, to become profitable but not at the expense of the planet. Brown got the title for her book, *Daring Greatly*, from a Teddy Roosevelt quote that says, "It's not the critic who counts; it's not the man who points out how the strong man stumbles or where the doer of deeds could've done it better. The credit belongs to the person who's actually in the arena, whose face is marred with blood and sweat and dust; who at the best in the end knows the triumph of high achievement, and who at worst, if he fails, he fails daring greatly."

Creativity is the number one quality needed in the business arena in the twenty-first century, for creativity at its roots is about choice, courage, commitment. It's about daring it, doing it, sharing it, and supporting others in the same process. It's about engagement, and that's what people are hungering for—engagement, purpose, meaning, value.

Cultural creatives are comfortable in this arena and have much to bring to a workplace environment, if only to redirect the conversation for a few hours. A recent study of millennials at work shows that they are "looking for a good work/life balance and strong diversity policies but feel that their employers have failed to deliver on their expectations." Another finding is that many of them feel "held back by rigid or outdated working styles." Corporate social responsibility values actually matter to millennials and "56% would consider leaving an employer who didn't have the values they expected."[23]

We are organisms in a constant state of flux, exposed to an ever-changing environment. Each of us is part of a system that is part of a larger system that is part of an even larger system. We are connected in integral ways. As the Nigerian chief says, "If you don't share your wealth with us, we will share our poverty with you."[24] Or as the Hassidic proverb puts it, "The trees, upon seeing the ax enter the forest, noticed its wooden handle and said 'Look, one of us.'"

As a civilization, we have shifted out of an industrial, assembly-line mindset of isolated units into an organic, knowledge-based network of communities. There is a tectonic shift of consciousness occurring and an evolutionary tendency away from the mechanical and back toward the natural. This may be seen as Mother Nature's midcourse correction. As the thinking neurons of the planet, biologically oriented toward survival, we are finding ways of connecting and communicating with unimaginable speed and precision. It has been calculated that we can globally transmit the contents of the Library of Congress across a single fiber optic line in 1.6 seconds.

This revolution in human consciousness is occurring at breakneck speed. So much information is coming our way that we are experiencing heightened levels of neural fatigue on a daily basis. It takes a new kind of creative leader to address the complexities and concerns facing the workforce today. Creative leadership calls for equal portions of humility and courage, introspection and outward action, self-awareness and self-transcendence. It is an art whose form is openness and whose function is service. Creative leaders take us back to our common roots and forward to our common needs. They do not hesitate to bring up our rights and responsibilities to each other as citizens of a great nation and planet. It is not the task of leaders to know the answers, but to articulate the questions we face as a people and to call us together to create our solutions.

There is a great potential now in corporate America—the chance to redesign structures and strategies to inspire, to become centers of creative ingenuity, arbiters of a culture that brings the whole human family into the picture. The profits from such an endeavor—materially, culturally, spiritually—could overwhelm the most skeptic imagination. Howard Bloom, author of *Global Brain* writes,

> Imagine what it would be like if at every staff meeting you were expected to put the care of the multitudes we mistakenly call "consumers" first. Imagine what it would be like to go to work each morning in a company that saw your passions as your greatest engines, your curiosities as your fuel, and your idealism as the pistons of your labors and of your soul. Imagine what it would be like if your superiors told you that the ultimate challenge was to tune your empathic abilities so you could sense the needs of your firm's customers even before those customers quite knew what they hankered after. [25]

People today are looking for meaning, for work that matters, for ways to be of use. We want our hearts to be engaged as much as our minds and hands, and this happens through relationships, in creative communities where the questions about what to produce and how to produce it are influenced by the deeper questions of what is needed and who needs it. It doesn't matter if you're the CEO of a multinational corporation, an inner-city teacher, a religious leader, or a traveling salesperson—you take in the world every day through your five senses and it is telling you something. You are hearing the needs of your community, your family, and your world on a daily basis, and the grand meaning you seek is directly related to your response to these needs.

Viktor Frankl, Holocaust survivor and author of *Man's Search for Meaning*, writes,

> We needed to stop asking about the meaning of life, and instead to think of ourselves as those who were being questioned by

life—daily and hourly. Our answer must consist, not in talk and meditation, but in right action and in right conduct. Life ultimately means taking the responsibility to find the right answer to its problems and to fulfill the tasks which it constantly sets for each individual.[26]

The tasks set for us now, as co-creators of this global civilization, are the tasks of doing no harm, of using the natural resources of our energy and creativity for the common good, and of uplifting the common person in whatever ways we can. These are the moral imperatives of this time, and creative leaders, or rather *successful* creative leaders, in all professions are incorporating these mandates in the agendas they are promoting. Right action and right conduct lead us directly to the right answers that Frankl refers to. We are not being naïve when we ask ourselves, *What is life asking of us today? What do we have to contribute? How can we make this offering in a way that sustains us as it enlivens others?*. We are not being liberal or conservative. We are opening ourselves to the greatest imaginative challenge, increasing our chances of success exponentially by matching our gifts—our creativity—with the urgent needs of our time.

This is the work that inspires greatness, engages the soul, and transforms the workplace from a labor camp to a laboratory of human possibility. I heard someone say the other day,

"We are not hungry for what we are not getting; we are hungry for what we are not giving." I think that's true.

As creative leaders, our work is to be clear in our own thinking processes. To be able to say, unequivocally, "These are the values that guide me. This is my personal bottom line. This is the impact I am making with my life." It's important for everyone in the workplace and the nonprofit space to come to terms with what we do with our time and energy. Who benefits? Who suffers?, What is the consequence of our existence? These are the questions that help us redirect, refocus if we have glazed over, gone off track, or happened into someone else's creation instead of our own. There is nothing complex about these questions. They do not call for genius, but rather for the ability to imagine the wake we are leaving in our path.

These are the questions that should be asked every day of each and every one of us.

- As a result of you being here, who is being served?
- Who feels more capable, more confident, because of your presence in their lives?
- What difference are you making?
- Where are you casting your light?
- What joy is being created out of your service?
- What deep desire do you have for your life?

We participate in our own evolution; we cause it to progress as we shape our lives around the answers to these questions. We find our purpose and the means to fulfill it at the place where our deepest desires meet the world's deep needs. This is the wellspring of our vitality—this intersection of self-awareness and self-giving.

CHAPTER 6

HEAL THYSELF: WHY CREATIVITY AND WELL-BEING GO HAND IN HAND

Art is not cozy and it is not mocked. Art tells the only
truth that ultimately matters. It is the light by which
human beings can be mended.
IRIS MURDOCH

ARTS TO THE RESCUE

THE PHONE RANG early in the morning. It was Ruth.

"This is a save-the-date call."

"What for?" I asked.

"I bought out the Town Square Theater for four showings. It's coming up this weekend. You have to see this film."

"You bought out a theater for four showings of what??"

"*Escape Fire: The Fight to Rescue American Health Care.*

"What's that?

"It's a documentary that exposes the sickness in our American health care system. And it's not just the movie. We have a panel of experts after every show. We've got integrative doctors, naturopaths, healers, and military officials. It's going to be an amazing dialogue. You have to be there."

"For sure I'll be there, but how'd you get involved in this? It's not quite your style."

"I was at a Think Tank in Maryland. The Samueli Institute was working with the military to come up with integrative health programs that could be leveraged and scaled."

"For what?"

"For the total well-being of military families and personnel, that's what. For the health and resilience of military folks and their families. It's a whole body-mind-spirit thing. There's a focus on vets, of course, but actually we're looking for solutions that apply to everyone."

Turns out, the producer who made the film *Escape Fire* needed grassroots help with its distribution and Ruth stepped up. She recently termed off the board but was on the Samueli Institute board for years in Alexandria, Virginia, along with several other national boards that deal with whole-person health, evidence-based science, and academic research on the delivery of compassionate health care in this country. Intimately familiar with the healing power of the arts, Ruth advocates for programs that engage participants in all things creative: brainstorming circles, storytelling, art making. This was her creative response to the Think Tank.

Not only did she buy out the theater for four showings, but also she helped assemble a team and spent a week inviting people to come for free. She involved the VA Services of San Diego, the naturopathic students of Bastyr University, medical, nursing and social work students at UCSD, leadership students from USD, officers from the Navy, the Army and the Marines, psychologists, and as many military families as she could get.

When Ruth introduced the film to the packed audience, she asked, "What it is that causes you to step out of your comfort zone and try something new, something you are unsure about? For me, it is when nothing I have tried has worked and I have no other available options. When I feel like my back is against the wall. That is usually when I say, 'Okay, I'll try anything.'"

She shared that 18 percent more soldiers died by suicide than were killed in combat. "The atrocities that our servicemen and women have seen and endured don't simply go away when they come home again.

Pharmaceuticals have long been the answer the government offers. The old solution was to suck it up like a good soldier, take the medication, and move on. But that's not working anymore," said Ruth.

In the documentary she was introducing, the directors Matthew Heineman and Susan Froemke follow a soldier from his battlefield injury in the Middle East to his release from Walter Reed Army Hospital many months later. During his time there, he was prescribed prescription drugs for pain, depression, insomnia, tremors, and anxiety by a number of different physicians from many different departments. Upon his release, he walked out of Walter Reed with 38 different prescriptions that he personally needed to manage.

How could anyone be equipped to take on the task of managing these drugs, much less an injured serviceman with PTSD and other undiagnosed conditions? An intervention in the form of complementary healing practices for his emotional well-being came his way in Walter Reed Hospital. Acupuncture, music, creative arts, visualization, and journaling were offered to him, and he reluctantly agreed because he had nowhere else to turn. He was surprised that after a couple of months, these practices combined with other more conventional approaches gave him some relief from his pain and mental anguish. He improved and was finally discharged and sent back home to Alabama.

When speaking with Matthew Heineman, the Marine confided, "I'm just a good 'ole boy from 'Bama who drinks beer and wrestles gators, and didn't know nuthin' about stuff like that."[1] But somehow those creative approaches worked for him. Visualization helped calm his mind. Music and drawing helped him express his feelings. Writing about his experience felt healing to him. This young Marine from Alabama had experienced first-hand the true meaning of art healing.

The usefulness of creativity to the healing process is thoroughly examined in a white paper titled "Arts, Health and Well-Being across the Military Continuum" by the National Initiative for Arts and Health in the Military.[2] The Walter Reed Bethesda campus is home to the National Intrepid Center of Excellence (NICoE), a 72,000-square-foot facility dedicated to advancing the clinical care, diagnosis, research, and education of service members and families experiencing combat related traumatic brain injury (TBI) and psychological health (PH) conditions. The Healing Arts Program at the NICoE integrates art into the patient's continuum of care, providing each individual with new tools in artistic and creative modalities—including creative writing, music, and visual art. The arts are incorporated to mitigate anxiety, enhance focus, and provide a nonverbal way for the veterans to express themselves and process traumatic experiences. Creative arts therapists at NICoE work with partners such as the National Endowment for the Arts' Operation Homecoming to expand artistic outlets for patients and their families.

The white paper looks at how humans have used the arts since the beginning of recorded history to help us learn, grow, and heal. Historically, humans have turned to the arts to express thoughts and reach a deeper understanding of ideas and feelings about our experiences. Our interest in the arts is lodged in our genes and in the genes of our ancestors who first painted cave walls and carved sculptures out of stone. It is a natural, general inclination that leads to beauty, elegance, order, and spontaneity. The arts that we have been exposed to have healed us, informed us, excited us, challenged us, and confronted us. Throughout the past and the immediate present, there is no denying the power of our creativity and its expression.

UNDERSTANDING CREATIVITY'S MAGICAL POWERS

When we are in the process of creating, we feel transported in time. We are engaged in the present moment, safely rooted in the now. There is no future to be anxious about, no past to resent. According to neuroscientist Kelly Lambert in her book *Lifting Depression,* when we do meaningful work with our hands, a neurochemical feedback floods our brains with dopamine and serotonin. Lambert explains that we have evolved to release these chemicals both to reward ourselves for working with our hands and to motivate ourselves to do it some more. She identifies a circuit in the human brain—connecting movement, feeling, and cognition—that is responsible for symptoms of depression and shows that when we knit a sweater, prepare a meal, or simply repair a lamp, we're actually bathing our brain in "feel-good" chemicals.

The National Endowment for the Arts (NEA) engaged in a nearly year long process of collaborative research inquiry that culminated in a theory of how art works as a system in America. The NEA uses the term "art" to include all of the arts. It is their belief that engagement in art contributes to quality of life, which contributes to society's capacity to invent, create, and express itself. A cyclical, working system results in expansion and deepening of arts engagement, enhanced quality of life, and an increase in society's creative capacity.

The positive impact of using creative arts therapies and art for therapeutic, educational, and expressive purposes in community settings is also encouraging. In addition to private for-profit and nonprofit health facilities, creative arts practitioners and creative arts therapists work across a wide spectrum of populations, serving persons from cradle to grave. A variety of reports, all noted in the white paper, cite research findings confirming that arts programming, creative arts therapies, and/or evidence-based design can

- build resilience,
- enhance patient coping,
- reduce length of hospital stays,
- decrease the need for pain medication,
- reduce patient levels of depression and situational anxiety,
- increase self-esteem,
- reduce health care-related infection rates,
- decrease the need for use of sedation during medical procedures, and
- increase patient satisfaction.[3]

Gail Rule-Hoffman, professor and program director of the Art Therapy and Counseling Department at Ursuline College in Cleveland, Ohio, spoke of the confusion that exists about various careers and professions involving a creative process and self-expression for healing. Arts and health practitioners encompass a multidisciplinary continuum that includes artists and performers, artists in health care, creative arts therapists, and health care professionals who integrate arts activities into their approved scope of practice. "While our students need to be licensed counselors as well as licensed art therapists, there are new programs cropping up all the time that have less rigid standards," said Rule-Hoffman. "Students can now get undergraduate degrees in Arts and Medicine which allow them to use creativity as a tool for healing, without going through the rigorous certification programs our students are involved with."[4]

The creative arts therapies include six specialties.

1. Art therapy – A mental health experience facilitated by a certified art therapist. Clients are encouraged to use creative processes to produce artwork that helps them explore their feelings, reconcile conflicts, grow in self-awareness, manage addictions, reduce anxiety, and increase self-esteem.
2. Music therapy – The use of music interventions by a credentialed professional who has completed an approved music therapy program. Individualized goals are established within a therapeutic relationship and music is a pathway to those goals.
3. Dance/movement therapy – Physical movement is used in psychotherapeutic situations to foster the emotional, cognitive, physical and social integration of the individual.
4. Poetry therapy – A practice that uses poetry and the language arts to help people clarify the roots of their conflicts, express their feelings, and transform crucial life issues.
5. Drama therapy –This therapeutic approach is more theatrical and experiential. Participants use drama to tell their stories, solve problems, express feelings. Through these experiences, their inner world can be actively explored. As individuals expand their repertoire of dramatic roles, they often come to understand more clearly their own life roles.

6. Psychodrama – Psychodrama is often used in a variety of clinical and community-based settings and group scenarios. Often used as a psychotherapy in which clients use spontaneous dramatization and role-playing to gain insight into their lives, this practice allows each person in the group to become therapeutic agents for each other. Psychodrama is not, however, a form of group therapy. It is an individual treatment protocol that takes place within a group.

Each discipline has professional training standards, a formal credentialing process, continuing education requirements, clinical practice standards, and a code of ethics. By combining psychotherapy and counseling with the healing power of creative expression and communication through the arts, each specialty is inherently interdisciplinary.

Increasingly, colleges and universities—such as Montgomery College, University of Buffalo, University of Florida, and University of Oregon—have joined arts organizations, including ArtStream, Smith Center for Healing and the Arts, The Creative Center, and health care institutions (e.g., Georgetown University Hospital's 20-year-old Studio G Artists in-Residence Program), in providing appropriate coursework for artists in health care. Through its College of Fine Arts, the University of Florida has a program in Arts in Health Care for undergraduate and graduate students and will soon offer a graduate degree in Arts and Health Care.

In September 2013, Americans for the Arts and the Sundance Institute in Utah invited Ruth to take part in their annual thirty-person roundtable. The focus of the three-day discussion was arts and healing. Their biographies were sent ahead of time so everyone had a chance to read and become familiar with each other's stories and work in advance. Once they were at the roundtable, the question was asked, "What is your earliest recollection of the creative process and art being the thing that defined you."

As you can see below, Ruth's answer was comprehensive and illustrative of how critical the arts can be to individual healing.

For the group, I recalled some of my story about being a latch-key kid, frightened and alone and using my drawing as a way to help me cope with a situation that young people shouldn't have to endure. Because I was alone so much of the time, I had to find ways to fill my time. I gravitated toward pencil and paper and began drawing objects I saw in my house. The first thing I worked on was a bowl of waxed fruit that sat decoratively on our kitchen table.

At six years old, I first tried to get the outlines of the shapes. The banana near the bottom of the bowl leaned horizontally against the white ceramic bowl. On top of the banana, the apples and oranges teetered, and at the top of the bowl were a group of cherries and small bunch of grapes. The hours turned into days and weeks of drawing and redrawing the same bowl of fruit arranged in exactly the same way. After I felt I'd mastered the shapes, I noticed shading or darkening on certain areas of the fruit and under the bowl, so I began to work on that

Weeks later, I had I moved from shading and to putting colors on the fruits and then a background around the fruits. By age seven, I had a rudimentary self-taught knowledge of drawing that I learned through trial and error. This pastime became the passion that still drives me today. Visual constructing and destructing became my problem solving technique that has crossed over into every area of my life.

Robert Redford, who was the co-sponsor of the event, was next in the circle to speak. "I'm just amazed," he said. "Ruth just told my whole story."[5] He, too, had been a latchkey kid who wasn't comfortable around other kids and wanted to do his own thing, which was drawing. He'd draw scenes of cowboys. Redford explained to the circle that the creative lens he has always looked through has defined him as a person. The skills and love for art he acquired as a child has directed his work in the areas of film, in the creation of the Sundance Institute, and in his environmental philanthropy. He is a talented painter, wood craftsman, and carpenter. He is thoughtful, caring, and grounded in his skin, believing that his creativity is not only the thing that sustained him, but that creativity is responsible for the trajectory his life has taken.

For both Robert Redford and Ruth, early immersions in the creative arts launched them into adult lives that are highly creative and original, socially conscious and community-oriented. Neither of them let in the notion that they weren't creative. They experienced creativity as a healing thing. It helped their fears go away. It comforted them and guided the trajectories of their lives.

However it happens, somewhere along the path, many of us come to believe the fallacy that creativity is an attribute of only a chosen few. We think if we're not producing artistic works, we are not creative. And that is the biggest hurdle of all, for we are the creators of these times, these cultures, these communities we live in. We hold the whole world in our hands, and if healing is needed, creativity is the very thing we should be engaging.

Creativity is not something that has to be worked at, but something that is released automatically when we are on the right paths, in our right minds. It is a force waiting to be released, inherent in each and every one of us. If we feel blocked in our creativity, perhaps we should take another look to see what inherited beliefs we are holding onto that keep us from our creative inclinations. Ask if this what you really wanted to create for your life? Are these really the choices that bring you joy, that resonate with who you are?

The creative act *sometimes* leads to painted canvases, poems, dramas and dances; it is sometimes married to the arts, but not always. Sometimes creativity is simply the act of transforming thoughts into experiences, words into events. It is about imagining, visioning, seeing the future we long for, then desiring it, speaking about it, feeling it until we actually become a strong enough gravitational force to bring it into being. Being that focused, that disciplined, that centered is a practice, a mindfulness practice, that keeps us whole, calm and grounded as we practice it. And that's what heals us. The state of mind that is the foundation for our creative work is the very thing that awakens our intuition and originality.

It may be frightening to think of reinventing your life, but consider the vast possibilities that may open up once you commit to a life that's in line with your true calling. Why not start from scratch and imagine what you would do if you had it to do all over again? To live creatively is to live from the soul, to shape our circumstances out of our deepest desires instead of conforming our dreams to the circumstances in which we find ourselves. Committing to our creativity is an act of faith, a promise that we will keep at it. Creativity is work of the heart. It is not about ego, not about money or success or failure.

In the work we create, the stories we tell, there is always the possibility that others will find some meaning they have been seeking, or some thrill of recognition may occur as they stand shoulder-to-shoulder with what we offer. In *Writing the Personal Essay,* poet Sheila Bender explains, "There are feelings and longings we understand and accept in ourselves only when we recognize them in someone else's words, words that have never been ours to speak until we saw them written out of someone else's life."[6]

Many of us are afraid to share what is deepest and most sacred in our lives. There is a hesitancy to speak first, to risk our private thoughts. So we hold them in, not even consciously, but simply because it's how we keep our composure. The deep intimacy we crave does not occur by default. We have to dare to expose ourselves to risk and vulnerability. But the prize is life changing, a total answer to our prayers. Creators in every medium have spoken of this process time and again.

Take for example, what John Ruskin wrote in his introduction to *Eudora Welty Photographs.*

The greatest thing a human soul ever does in this world is to *see* something, and tell what it saw in a plain way. Hundreds of people can talk for one who can think, and thousands can think for one who can see. To see clearly is poetry, philosophy, and religion, all in one.[7]

The Hebrew Kabbalah puts it another way. "We receive the light, then we impart it. Thus we repair the world." And this doesn't mean feeling an absence of fear, being on fire with inspiration, brimming with cocky confidence. Georgia O'Keeffe admitted she was "absolutely terrified every moment of my life and I've never let it keep me from doing a single thing I wanted to do."[8] In *Bird by Bird*, Anne Lamott counsels, "Even if only the people in your writing group read your memoirs or stories or novel, even if you only wrote your story so that one day your children will know what life was like when you were a child and you knew the name of every dog in town—still, to have written your version is an honorable thing to have done."[9]

In our research survey on creativity, Ruth and I asked our participants about the healing power of creativity. Respondents cited their personal experiences as having been overwhelmingly positive in this regard.

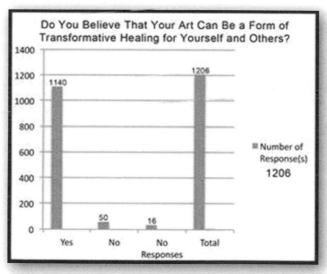

Phillips/Westreich Creativity Survey, 2014. (PW003)[10]

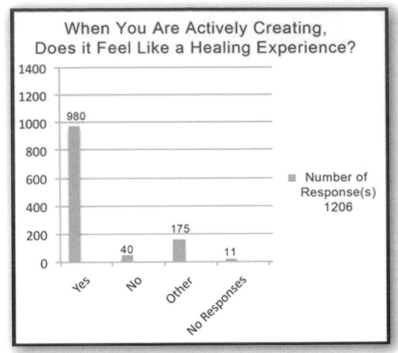

Phillips/Westreich Creativity Survey, 2014 (PW004)

OVERCOMING COMMON OBSTACLES TO HEALING

While respondents acknowledged that the act of creating can heal, this next set of data reveals an interesting complication; many of us hesitate to create because we fear imperfection or don't feel our work is good enough or valuable to anyone.

Ping Ho is founding director of UCLArts and Healing, an organization that teaches community members how to facilitate healing experiences through the arts. Some of its programs include the Social Emotional Arts Certificate Program and its evidence-based *Beat the Odds: Social and Emotional Skill Building Delivered in a Framework of Drumming.* Ho explains,

> The arts have innate therapeutic benefits that make them uniquely well suited to facilitate social and emotional well-being.

The process of creative expression without expectations of mastery enables us to externalize what is within, and can enhance positive emotions besides reducing negative ones. The universal appeal and nonverbal elements of the arts enable anyone to participate, without the stigma of therapy or the side effects of pharmaceuticals.[11]

Ho believes that shared arts experiences deepen possibilities for empathy, dialogue and finding meaning in life experience. In speaking of her experience at UCLArts, she says:

Reflection on the process of creative expression can reveal the self and facilitate connection to others in a way that feels safe and organic. Tears are often shed when members of the community read aloud what they have written or hear what someone else has written. Often people share a trauma that they have never shared with anyone before, only to discover that others in the room have had the same experience. Within the space of an hour, a roomful of strangers can become each other's closest confidantes.[12]

Ho tells the story of a diminutive and somewhat disheveled woman named Rosa, who sat in the corner with her head down the whole time during the first session of a program called "Awakening from Trauma through Breath, Sound, and Movement." At the end of the first session, she told instructor and trauma expert Carolyn J. Braddock that she didn't think she learned anything because she was dissociating the whole time, which is a form of mental detachment that is characteristic of trauma.

Carolyn reassured her that she'd probably learned more than she thought she did and to see what she might remember the next morning. "Rosa telephoned us to say that she had indeed remembered some of the tai chi movements that she had been taught, which in combination with her own yoga practice helped to give her the presence of mind to hang up on her abusive husband for the first time in her life," recounts Ho.

In the second session, Rosa tried to tell her story to the group, but choked on her words, another common characteristic of trauma. Tears streamed down her face, without even the faintest sound. Carolyn knelt down to her level, held her hands asked her to breathe, and then asked her to let out a sound with the breath any sound. Rosa did. Next, she asked Rosa to walk with her and feel the ground beneath her feet; this was a way to physically ground her and keep her in the present moment.

After that, Carolyn asked Rosa to lead some movements with her arms that Carolyn would follow. Ho explains,

> When someone mirrors or builds on our ideas or actions, we are seen and heard. Mirroring can be as simple as eye contact or as complex as the 'yes-and' principle in theater, whereby one always accepts and builds on a line or action delivered to them. This is a form of empathy. Synchrony is a major principle through which the arts have their healing benefits.[13]

In a matter of minutes, Rosa was able to share her lifetime of rage over having been forced by her culture to marry her rapist and have children by him.

A week or so later, Rosa called to say that she was starting to experience intense feelings, from which the dissociation had protected her earlier. She wondered what she should do. "I asked what made her feel good," reflects Ho. "She said listening to music, so I encouraged her to do that. Listening to music that one likes activates areas of the brain associated with reward and pleasure. Carolyn also suggested that she kick and scream in a pool."[14]

Two months after the five-session trauma program ended, Ho saw Rosa again at another one of their programs, "Sustainable Movement 24/7." Ho recalls,

She waltzed in, glowing. Her hair was styled nicely in a flip and she made eye contact with those around her. She was smiling and touching people. She bore no resemblance to the Rosa that I had known earlier. It was amazing to witness her transformation. The management of trauma, which can typically be a lengthy process, seemed to be greatly facilitated by simple and accessible, arts-based tools. That's public health at its best.[15]

Rachel Naomi Remen, a well-known pioneer in the field of integrative medicine, writes in *Kitchen Table Wisdom: Stories That Heal,* "At the deepest level, the creative process and the healing process arise from a single source. When you are an artist, you are a healer; a wordless trust of the same mystery is the foundation of your work and its integrity." As a doctor with a sixty-year personal history of Crohn's disease, she brings the perspective of both physician and patient. Self-care and healing comes for Rachel when she is creating art and journaling as well as using forms of yoga to integrate the mind, body, and spirit.

Remen writes,

You may think of self-care as something that distracts you from the interesting and creative aspects of your life – time consuming but necessary, like needing to change the oil in your car every 5,000 miles. Many of us – especially those with an orientation to service – are accustomed to overriding our own needs. But, the real truth is that self-care is a practice that can draw us closer to the sanctity of life. [16]

Those of us who have art in our souls and have used art as a therapeutic healing tool throughout our lives understand its value at the deepest level. Although a relatively new concept in western society—with the emergence of professions in creative-arts therapy over the last sixty years—health professionals, therapists, and others in the medical field have begun to acknowledge the therapeutic effects of art and music on the physical, emotional, and mental well-being of people. [17]

Rachel Remen, MD, was not afraid to step out of her comfort zone within a conventional medical community and say, as both physician and patient, she needed practices and tools that she herself could use for self-care. And after acknowledging that, she went about finding them and integrating them into her work and practice for more than forty years. Remen has founded wellness organizations such as The Institute for the Study of Health & Illness (ISHI), a professional training institute providing education and support for health professionals at all levels of training.

Another professional determined to incorporate the arts into his practice is New York social worker Dan Cohen. In 2006, Cohen, realized that all of his favorite music was at his fingertips with today's devices, but he might no longer be able to listen to it if he winds up in a nursing home with Alzheimer's. His initial research in 2006 showed that out of 16,000 nursing homes and assisted-living facilities, none provided their patients with iPods.[18] Cohen started a non-profit project known as Music & Memory, which distributes iPods and helps seniors living in nursing homes access to the songs of their youth.

The power of music and song is deeply embedded in our psyche. Alzheimer's disease is progressive and eventually terminal, so the goal is simply to connect patients with an aspect of the past that still burns bright, even as the present becomes increasingly dim. "The music from their youth is still preserved, and that awakens them," Cohen said. "You're bypassing the failed short-term cognition, but their emotional state is still there."[19] One of the patients could no longer speak or recognize his daughter, but after listening to an iPod loaded with songs by Cab Calloway, he came to life. He started singing along and talking about being filled with love and romance.

Oliver Sachs, MD, a British-born neurologist, is an expert in music and memory. He is also the author of the book *Awakenings* that was later adapted into a film starring Robert DeNiro and Robin Williams.

In the documentary film, *Alive Inside,* based on Sachs' book, Cohen states, "Music connects people with who they have been, who they are and their lives, because what happens when you get old is all the things you're familiar with, your identity, they're all just being peeled away."[20] In *Musicophilia: Tales of Music and the Brain,* Sachs explores the relationship humans have with music, its power over us and through us, as well as how music can help access those unreachable emotional states of those people suffering with Alzheimer's and other neurological diseases. He writes, "Music, uniquely among the arts, is both completely abstract and profoundly emotional. It has no power to represent anything particular or external, but it has a unique power to express inner states or feelings. Music can pierce the heart directly; it needs no mediation." [21]

In a rigorous research study in 2010, Justin Feinstein, Melissa Duff and Daniel Tranel explored how emotions that are altered by music can remain long after the memory of having listened to the music is gone. They studied how sustained experience of emotion remained present even after loss of memory in patients with amnesia. Their conclusions were that emotions linger after memory fades. [22]

We interviewed San Diego-based expert in music wellness and music therapy Barbara Reuer, PhD. Reuer manages direct music therapy services to children with special needs, medical patients, and hospice patients, as well as facilitating groups dealing with substance abuse, eating disorders, cancer, lifestyle change, and bereavement. She spoke of the Resounding Joy Semper Sound Military Music Therapy program, which was started in 2010 to provide integrative treatment for service members experiencing trauma. It serves active duty service members, families, and veterans throughout San Diego County at military installations and at the VA Aspire Center, a residential treatment facility for combat veterans. The program runs a weekly, 90-minute progressive music therapy group and offers individual adaptive instruction, incorporating both music and therapy. In 2014, Resounding Joy established a satellite program serving veterans in Massachusetts. They also operate

Healing Notes for Children, Mindful Music for Seniors, and Sound Minds for Young Families in addition to Semper Sound.

Reuer shared two anecdotes to show the positive impact Semper Sound is having on veterans: These are her words, as told to Ruth:

Meet Jay, a Navy Corpsman, deployed multiple times to Iraq and Afghanistan. He experienced IED blasts causing traumatic brain injury and post-traumatic stress, leading to substance abuse, isolation, and several attempts at ending his life. But then he found Semper Sound. He found hope, a reason to live. Music therapy sessions built a bridge to communication and helped to lessen his pain. He is now attending music college and proclaims proudly, "Music Therapy saved my life."

Next is Tom, a Marine Corps instructor who fell 110 feet out of a helicopter during training exercises. This accident left him in a coma for 30 days and caused a catastrophic brain injury. While in a coma, his wife gave birth to their little girl. Tom requires constant care and cannot live with his wife and daughter. Music is a vehicle for communication. Writing songs allows his family a window into his soul, and helps him connect to his daughter. Recording and selling his music also provides some economic empowerment. Both Jay and Tom reconnected to their families, communities, and most importantly, themselves through the power of music.[23]

Much of this kind of research has been conducted with advanced Parkinson's patients and music. Enrico Fazzini, MD, a neurologist at New York University Medical Center explains, "The effectiveness of music therapy is linked to what Parkinson's disease takes away from patients: their ability to move automatically. A lot of times Parkinson's patients can dance beautifully when they can't walk. I have people who can barely take a step, but they can dance. Because they bring the unconscious into the conscious." [24]

Each of our powerful senses of smell, sound, taste and vision transport us. They evoke memories, images, stories. Engaging our senses can be used to great effect in pain management. Most people, skilled or not in art, have experienced how creative practices can transform their states of mind. Whether we're engaging actively or passively—making art or appreciating art—*something* happens. A painting might make you feel nostalgic or comforted, a piece of music can cheer you up or quiet you down. A poem or a photograph can alter your thoughts, raise your consciousness, move you to action.

Imagery, or visualization, is one of medicine's oldest and most meditative tools. In healing rituals and ceremonies, imagery of dreams and visions have been used for centuries. Modern medicine, with all the emphasis on new technologies and curing of disease, seems to have forsaken healing tools of the past. But in the last couple of decades, there has been increasing interest in more holistic approaches to healing, including guided imagery, arts, music, and storytelling.

Columbia University College of Physicians and Surgeons offers a program in Narrative Medicine, started by Rita Charon, MD, who took a PhD in English when she realized the importance of storytelling to the work of doctors and patients. She has published and lectured extensively on the ways in which narrative training increases empathy and reflection in health care providers. In an article by Gina Kolata in the *New York Times* Education Life section, Dr. Charon explained how "through literature, she learned how stories are built and told, and translated that to listening to, and better understanding, patients."[25] Dr. Charon devised techniques to help patients understand and share their own stories and then created ways for health professionals to solicit these stories and comprehend them as part of the larger narrative of the patients' lives.

Dr. Charon directs the Narrative Medicine curriculum for Columbia University and teaches literature, narrative ethics, and life telling, both in the medical center and Columbia's Department of English. Talk about marrying the creative arts and healing. We, as a people, are evolving into a higher level of consciousness. We are seeing the value of what's within, finding the healing power inside our own stories, just as the Amazonian tribes have found the medicine that lies before them in the leaves and plants of their own rainforest. Each of us contains much of the medicine that will heal us, but unless it is released or expressed, it cannot do its job.

That's where creativity comes in. Creativity is the breaking open of the healing balm. It's the release of the feelings, the memories, and the stories that help heal us. It's the community of listeners, the solidarity of our chosen families, that helps us feel valued as part of a whole.

I had lunch with a friend who has worked for years as a writer and editor for elders wanting to create legacy books before they die. She interviews each person, records their memories, then transcribes, edits, and publishes the stories so that each individual can actually see and touch what felt like the meaning of their lives. When I asked her if she was still doing that work, she responded, "Yes, but there's been an interesting change. I'm not making so many books now. Most times, I'm just listening. They hire me not to write their book, but to witness their memories. They just want someone to *hear* them. That's what heals them in some way." We know this to be true in the ordinariness of our lives and in the organizations we have created. There is no denying it. Having someone witness our story can be an amazing healing event.

According to Annie Heiderscheit, PhD at the Center for Spirituality and Healing at the University of Minnesota, using a creative arts modality in her program allows her to assist patients in discovering and experiencing their own innate abilities to heal. Ruth first met Heiderscheit in 2012 when she was invited to experience the program firsthand and participate in a drumming circle. This was Ruth's first foray into drumming and she wasn't quite sure what to expect.

"I didn't know anything about playing the drums," said Ruth. "There must have been twenty different kinds of drums and percussion instruments. Everyone sat in a big circle, chose an instrument, and waited. Then we began playing whatever we had in our hands and the cacophony of sounds that lasted for a long time." With no one directing them, they found themselves playing together at times, then separately, then back together again.

"At the end, I felt a kind of peaceful, lingering high, and I was not the only one," said Ruth. "We talked about it after, and everyone in the room felt they had been touched and changed in a noticeable way. It was hard to articulate the feeling exactly, but it was truly healing"

The process of expressing ourselves creatively is cathartic and creates physiological changes in the body similar to that of meditation. Studies show that music therapy can lower heart rate and blood pressure and restore neurological function.[26] Art making and music making can provide relief from physical suffering. While the number of studies of the physiological effects of creative processes is small and represented largely by single case or small group studies, the most rigorous scientific studies (randomized, controlled trials, meta-analyses, and reviews) of the biological effects of arts-based interventions shows a distinct pattern of stress reduction.

For example, research shows that creative experiences increase the blood flow to the brain. This results in a more relaxed state. Deepak Chopra and his associates found that enjoyable creative activity gives rise to an α-wave pattern on an EEG typical of a relaxed but aware state of mind called restful alertness (also found in meditation).[27] Creative activities not only enhance brain functioning, they also increase serotonin, a chemical known to decrease feelings of depression.

According to the field of psychoneuroimmunology, stress-reducing and support-building practices improve our health and resistance to disease. The U.S. Military is researching complementary therapies that may help soldiers returning from duty cope better with post traumatic stress disorder (PTSD) and traumatic brain disorders (TBI) rather than always turning to pharmaceuticals.

As of 2014 more military service men and women die from suicide than died in combat.[28] This is not merely a national disgrace. It shows we are not meeting the health care and rehabilitation needs of our returning veterans. But new studies on engagement in the arts are demonstrating positive effects in sleep behavior, impulse control, and concentration among vets. Engagement in these programs are also proving to be more beneficial than pharmaceuticals in treating depression and anxiety. Veterans who have opportunities to express themselves and share their stories cope better with the most serious effects of today's conflicts and their suicide rates go down.

By serving as a protective and safe vehicle for veterans' emotions associated with combat, the arts are showing promise in mitigating the most tragic consequences of war—homelessness, suicide, and depression. Often, traumatic experiences are imprinted in the brain in such a way that they are not easily accessed through language. Creative and expressive arts therapies offer different ways for veterans to tap into and transform events that have compromised their well-being.

One program combining a variety of creative arts approaches is Valor Home, (www.valorhome.org.) in northeastern Ohio, which is working with 140 veterans at seven sites. Valor Home is a housing program of Family & Community Services that has been offering supportive, therapeutic housing for homeless and at-risk veterans in four counties since 2005. Their only model of care is expressive arts psychotherapies, and all of their employees are credentialed art therapists. "Talk therapy doesn't work well for vets," according to founder David Peacock, a Board-certified drama therapist who has worked with vets, addicts, and trafficked children for decades here and abroad. His wife, Lisa, also Board-certified as a drama therapist, incorporates poetry, narrative art, dance, and movement therapy to be sure the vets "have a whole body experience in connecting their heads to their hearts and bodies." [29]

They shared their approach in a recent phone interview. "It's so organic here, people don't think of it as a homeless shelter," said Peacock. "It's more like a health spa. We have classical music playing. We use lavender, chamomile, lilac and different kinds of aromatherapy. We painted the rooms in colors that would relax the brain. We grow much of our own food and consider good nutrition part of our therapy. And every day we begin with twenty minutes of mindfulness practice." [30]

Valor Home has a seven-therapist team, all of whom are dedicated to drawing the stories and suffering out of the vets in creative ways, so they have something to reframe, re-imagine, and transform. Says Lisa Peacock, "I create collaborative experiences for the vets and their families so they can use different media to tell their stories and find peace."[31]

Further south, Austin-based Darden Smith, a singer-songwriter, is putting his creativity to good use. Founder of the Be An Artist Program, Smith's most recent project, *Songwriting With: Soldiers*, evolved after he wrote "Angel Flight," a song honoring U.S. soldiers who have died in combat. The song was awarded a Public Service Medal by the Texas National Guard. *Songwriting With: Soldiers* was created with the goal of helping active duty and veteran U.S. soldiers returning from duty with PTSD and other emotional illnesses.

Smith works with soldiers on telling their stories through song. His idea is pairing professional songwriters with military members in a retreat setting. Smith was at the Sundance Roundtable with Ruth, and he shared with the group that he creates a collaborative environment focusing on listening and building trust. Together, a soldier and songwriter weave his or her personal experience into a song, taking the soldier's words and improvising a melody to match their stories.

From invisible battle scars to a spouse's isolation to the surge of adrenaline before a dangerous patrol, the resulting songs are as diverse as the participants themselves. The songs are recorded with the soldiers for them to take home and share with their families and beyond. "The songs pretty much write themselves," says Smith. "You just ask them questions and let them talk. They will give you the story."[32]

During the course of Ruth's time at the National Arts Policy Roundtable, Smith shared many stories and videos showing the impact his program has had on these returning soldiers and their families. One story stood out. FSS A. J. Merrifield, a former soldier who attended the *Songwriting with: Soldier's* workshop, says, "I have seen what it is like to lose your family," meaning his fellow soldiers. "What could ever prepare you to be away from home, death surrounding you all the time, watching your fellow buddies, who become your family, die horrific deaths?"

They return home and try to pick up the pieces of their lives but as Merrifield says, "Because of our experiences, we find ourselves feeling marginalized on the edges of the world, with a gulf that exists between us and those we know and care for. That gulf exists because we lack a way to communicate what we're truly thinking and feeling." [33]

That's why the expressive arts and creative programs are helping these vets and any other human being who needs help putting thoughts and feelings into words. It's hard enough to do that without being traumatized, but add the weight of trauma or brain injury to the equation and communication is seriously compromised. Up until now, as a culture, we have put creativity into a small box. We have associated it with art, painting, dance, singing, performing. But the work being done today in the creative arts is expanding that definition to include the narrative of our lives.

Stepping into the caverns of our own stories calls for courage and humility. To make a story of our choices, our paths, our failings, our hopes—*that* is an act of creation, a work of consequence. If we see you trying to do that, our own confidence builds steam. If we hear you say how it went down, what you lost, where you despaired, why you survived, that bolsters us in our own missions. In *The Wounded Storyteller,* Arthur Frank writes, "To tell one's own story, a person needs others' stories."[34]

It is not simply self-serving that we mine the stories of our lives. When we search for the jewels certain to be found at the depths of our personal wanderings, we can make sense of our moves, evaluate our choices, analyze our motivations, and determine what needs to shift to alter the course. Ruth's story illustrates how our stories are healing for us and healing for others.

I don't think I can count or remember how many times in my life I have relied on my creativity and my art to help heal my body, mind, and spirit. In the late 1980s, I was coming to the end of a long-term marriage, caring for a mother who was near the end of her life, all while trying to raise two children. I heard the term "sandwich generation" and I had the visual of me between two pieces of oversized bread, being suffocated as the bread closed in with me inside. One of the main reasons I left my marriage was that my health had been so compromised. I had chronic ulcers brought on by taking so many aspirin to help me cope with chronic joint and muscle pain brought on by years of chronic stress. Conventional doctors had done everything they could to help me, including all kinds of experimental ulcer drugs, so much so that my immune system became very compromised. They all agreed that unless I could lower my stress, there was nothing else they could do for me. In those years, they were fairly limited in what they had to prescribe.

My early painting career was in drawing, oils, and some watercolors. Then I put those aside and somewhere during my marriage, I turned to painting antique porcelain dishes similar to what one of my paternal relatives had painted. At the time, it felt like a medium I could handle. I studied and painted those porcelains for more than fifteen years. Each of the pieces sometimes had fifteen or more fires in my kilns. Some of the pieces were so intricate that I had to use a magnifying glass and a brush with just a few hairs to achieve the photorealism type results that the old porcelain masters such as Sevres and Dresden were able to achieve.

As I began the next chapter of my life, reducing my stress was my goal. I also felt a need to explore my creativity and artistic ability even more than I had in in early years. I was introduced to Ron Pekar, a well known sculpture, painter and teacher. I began taking painting lessons from him and he quickly became my mentor. He looked at my body of work, including my porcelains and made a request of me. I can still remember the conversation as though it were yesterday. He said that painters paint. That is what makes great painters. He was speaking about the

10,000-hour rule that Malcolm Gladwell wrote about in Outliers and that we discussed in chapter one.

He felt I was about twenty years behind in building my body of abstract organic work begun earlier in my painting career. But the big caveat was that in order to free myself from the constraints I had been working under, he wanted me to only create pieces that were at least as tall as I was. So that meant to paint nothing smaller than about five feet. That was a tall order for me, both emotionally and physically, as I didn't have a proper art studio and ended up painting in my garage on the floor. But it worked. After my first pieces, I became comfortable painting on the large canvases and painted some of my best work ever. I could feel the knots in my belly start to loosen, and within about six weeks, my ulcers went away. After that, I truly understood and believed there was such a strong connection between my body and mind. I could help in the healing process of my physical body by mitigating my stress level. Ron went on to mentor me through some of my most productive painting years.

In an article for the *Croatian Medical Journal,* neuroscientist Lukasz M. Konopka of the Loyola Medical Center writes about the marriage of art and neuroscience.[35] Originally, art therapy used pure art concepts, void of scientific inquiry. Now, slowly, it is embracing scientific thinking by using abundant neuroscientific data and the objective tools of scientific investigation. For years, we recognized that art-making allowed one to reframe experiences, reorganize thoughts, and gain personal insights that often enhanced one's quality of life. Konopka writes:

Art therapy has gained popularity because it combines free artistic expression with the potential for significant therapeutic intervention... Treating human pathology using art gives us a tremendous alternative unique and novel option for engaging brain networks that enhance the way the brain processes information, incorporates external and internal data, and develops new efficient brain connections. Our goal is for humans to become better adapted to their defined environments. [36]

Creativity heals us because it helps us process the past and call forth the future we hope to live into. It heals us because we are made whole as we weave together the fragments of our lives. It is an act that marries brain and heart, mind and body. Creativity roots us in the safety of the present moment, for it is not possible to create when one is lost in the land of *what was* or *what will be*. When we are grounded in the now, we breathe more deeply, think more clearly. Like a tree rooted in the earth, we draw up sustenance from below and take in broadcasts from above, as Emily Dickinson described in her beautiful line:

The only news I know
Is bulletins all day
From Immortality.[37]

Creativity is the human enterprise we were born for. We become most alive, most awake, and most aware when we engage in creative endeavors, whether it's the making of art or the making of our lives. The more conscious we are, the more beautiful the creation, the more extraordinary the life. The keys to our personal masterpiece are truly in our hands, our minds, our hearts.

CHAPTER 7

GET YOUR OWN STORY STRAIGHT: WHY YOUR PERSONAL NARRATIVE IS SO IMPORTANT

In a room where people unanimously maintain a conspiracy
of silence, one word of truth sounds like a pistol shot.
CZESLAW MILOSZ

OUR CREATIVITY IS SHAPED BY HOW WE LIVE OUR LIVES

I LEARNED HOW to speak from a man who didn't know how to listen. At least that was my perspective. I was hired as a part-time PR consultant for a non-profit company. My job was to write and produce their monthly newsletter, but when the CEO learned I was also a photographer and grant writer, he tasked me with writing a federal grant and taking the photos for the annual report.

Since it was my job to write his monthly letter to the employees, it felt important to me to get a sense of who he was, to get a feel for his voice and what he cared about. This was nearly impossible, because who he was—or perhaps more accurately, *what he was*—was inaccessible, emotionally speaking. I could not establish a relationship with him. He was a fact man, not a feeling man, and our styles of communication were like night and day.

My expectation was that we would engage in a dialogue every now and then—that there would be a back and forth of ideas, a process of unfolding our thoughts and feelings about different things so I could actually absorb and share the visions he held for the company. But he couldn't go there. There was a disconnect between his head and his heart. He could go on and on about numbers, but the subject of values was off limits.

When I needed his help prioritizing whether to meet the printing deadline for the annual report or the application deadline for a grant, he became infuriated if I mentioned my stress over the time pressures. "I don't want to know what you feel," he'd shout. "Just tell me what you need." I'd stutter and stammer, trying to get clear about the precise information I needed, but it was an alien way of communicating. I was a process person trying to do business with a product person, and the results might have been disastrous had I not converted to his way.

Within weeks, I had learned to silence my emotions, stifle my instincts, and curb my desire for creative interaction. I learned how to speak in bullets, to eliminate adjectives, to relate facts and findings without hope for any dialogue, and all our communications were crystal clear and highly efficient. I got the $750,000 grant, wrote and designed the annual report, spun out compelling media releases for a year, and then I quit, because my own creative fire was starting to smolder.

My creativity gets sparked in communion with others, not in isolation. While I do my writing in private, my thoughts are often conceived in public conversations. They are the product of community. The stories that we share are born in relationships. It is human interaction that gives us the narrative arc, the conflict, the denouement of all the tales we weave and tell. Our souls invite epic adventures to provide grist for our creative work. Every creative work we produce contains elements of our personal experience, whether it comes out in a minor chord, a balletic adagio, a comedic screenplay. Our story is the beginning, the seed of it all. As one writer once suggested, anyone who has survived childhood has enough material for several novels.

The sociologist Robert Bellah wrote, "Narrative is more than literature. It is the way we understand our lives." Our stories define us. They affect our well-being, our relationships, our present and our future. They are vehicles of energy, vessels of possibility. We can harness great light and power from the adventures of our lives, but first we must learn to harvest them. Just as a combine makes its way through a field, reaping, threshing and winnowing the grain from the chaff, so do we traverse the fields of our lives reaping and winnowing the kernels we have sown.

Though it may seem life is happening to us in a haphazard way, on some level we have cultivated the seeds for the stories that enfold us. Our thoughts become our words become our desires become our experience. We cannot shake a fist at fate without also acknowledging our role in its unraveling. Whatever experience comes our way, it happens both *to* us and *for* us. The best storytellers in the world are the people who have figured out not just *what* happened, but *why* and what it *gave* to them. They are the real goldminers, striking it rich by finding a nugget of insight in every unfolding.

Our bodies are the temples of our wisdom. Every cell holds a memory of what has happened. With our intuition, we can tap into the insights that crystallize in the darkness as we trudge through it. Every catastrophe or trauma strips us of something and gives us something. The nakedness, we know. The gifts are yet to be unearthed. "The story reveals the meaning of what would otherwise be an intolerable event," writes Hannah Arendt. The story helps us grasp the bigger picture. When we are able to dissect the experience by seeing it in story form, or distance ourselves enough from the event's sharp edges to see both the beginning and end of it, then we can view it as a survivor. We can identify the tumult, the turbulence we lived through—we can name it and know it as the price we paid for wisdom on our evolutionary journey.

But the wisdom doesn't come as a result of simply bearing the pain. Wisdom comes in the process of mastering the ordeal, understanding its complexity, seeing it not only from the perspective of the subject, but from the perspective of creator as well. Rachel Naomi Remen writes, "Stories can be understood as a form of testimony: testimony is initiated by suffering, and suffering comes to understand itself by hearing its own testimony."

When we train ourselves to see both sides of the story, we create new neural networks in our brain. We expand our consciousness, amplify our intuition. Meditation, or mindfulness practice, actually has an impact on the way our brains work. Neuroscientist Zoran Josipovic has discovered that depending on the focus of the meditation, different structures of the brain are activated. Non dual awareness meditation, or awareness of awareness, minimizes the strong subject-object dichotomy we usually experience. [1] It also causes a simultaneous sense of internal and external space. The more awareness we bring to the table, the less constrained we are by dualistic concepts like right and wrong, good and bad, black and white.

It is an evolutionary leap to transcend duality, to look at the whole instead of the parts, to see beyond the differences into the commonness of our experience. It is evolutionary to stretch ourselves to make a case for both sides, to re-pair the opposites, to see the value in our opponent's argument. It is a sign of true mastery that one can remain calm in the midst of emotional turbulence, or refrain from blame when things go wrong. As Baudelaire said, "True genius is the ability to hold two contradictory thoughts without losing your mind."

Lillian Smith, a Southerner and civil rights advocate who was born before women had the right to vote, addresses this in her book, *The Journey:*

> The artist knows something else, wordless, oftentimes, but he knows it deep within him: that were it not for the struggle and the loneliness he undergoes in his search for integrity there would be no strength or beauty in his work. And though art is not for the sake of beauty, *beauty must be there or the profound revelation the artist makes would be unbearable.* (italics mine)
>
> The artist in us knows, the poet in us knows: it is the mark not of ordeal but of mastered ordeal that gives a face, a life, a great event, or a great work of art its style. The wound is there, but the triumph also, the death and the birth, the pain and the deep satisfactions: it is all there in delicate equilibrium, speaking to us. [2]

As we evolve ourselves beyond our notions of right and wrong and contemplate the complexities that this world presents, we increase the bandwidth of our imagination. We stimulate our creative juices and our native intelligence. Shifting into non-dualistic thinking dissolves the boundaries between self and other. It lifts our awareness from mental to mystical. Our capacity for reception from Intelligence-at-Large improves a hundredfold. The signals become noise-free, static-free.

The stories of people who think beyond the poles contain deep wisdom. They are more compelling, less judgmental. They are loftier and transcendent. That is the training for genius: to practice the discipline of non-dual thinking. Toning our genius muscles is an act of will. It is like yoga for the soul. It's a constant practice of seeing both sides, taking both sides, surrendering our opinions over and over again as we let go of thought processes that have dominated us for eons. It is a mental practice, like Hafiz writes about in his poem, *"Why Aren't We Screaming Drunks?"* translated by Daniel Ladinsky:

> The sun once glimpsed God's true nature
> And has never been the same.

> Thus that radiant sphere
> Constantly pours its energy
> Upon this earth
> As does He from behind
> The veil.

> With a wonderful God like that
> Why isn't everyone a screaming drunk?

> Hafiz's guess is this:

> Any thought that you are better or less
> Than another

Quickly
Breaks the wine
Glass.[3]

Any thought that we are better or less than another quickly breaks the wine glass.
That says it all. To keep our wine glass intact involves a rigorous discipline. Just as holding two contradictory thoughts in your mind simultaneously does. Tending to that discipline is the very thing that changes the brain. Being conscious about your own thoughts and thinking thoughts that tend toward oneness is the practice that creates new neural networks, which is exactly what gets us out of the ruts of old thinking, old habits, old behaviors.

When you begin this practice—the practice of not thinking you are better or less than another—don't even try and make it through one day. See if you can get through one or two hours without comparing yourself to another. Try standing behind someone in a grocery line with a cart full of junk food and see if you can keep from being smug or judgmental. Try listening to a great speaker or storyteller and see if you can keep your own confidence at full tilt. Try it on the freeway for thirty miles at rush hour.

This kind of mind discipline is remedial work for great storytellers. They go over the events, deciding what to include and what to delete. They ponder where the story starts and where it ends. The decide on the main characters, reflect on the narrative arc, the climax, the resolution, and the moral of the story, if there is one. And over the years, our stories change. As we evolve, we become less and less the victim and more and more the protagonist, the hero, the change agent.

THE MANY SIDES OF TELLING A STORY

I spoke with a friend yesterday who's recovering from breast cancer. I've known her for thirty years. When I asked how she was doing, she said, "Well, I'm learning how to get my story right."

"Remember that story about me hunting with my father when I was a teen?" she asked. "The one where I had my .22 rifle and Dad went up ahead with the dog to flush out some quail?"

"Yes, I remember. You got stuck in some kind of quicksand."

"Well I just figured out I've been telling the story wrong all these years. I've always told it like it was about me being left alone. Like my father left me and I was a victim. But the truth is, I figured out how to get out of the swamp. I threw my gun onto the shore. I lay down horizontally in the muddy water. I stretched out and grabbed onto a reed that I could use to pull myself in, and I saved myself. The story isn't about being left alone. It's a story of me saving myself. It's a great story!"

And it was. It had power. It was about being a winner, not a victim. It was not a *poor-me* story, but a *Wow! Look what I did* story. And as the retelling lifted her up, it lifted me up right along beside her.

I shared a story with her that I had just learned to re-spin as well. "Remember that story about me being sent home from the convent? How devastated I was, and with no plan B? Nowhere to go and no idea how to make a life? Remember what a sad story it was, how I always cried and thought I'd never get over it?"

"It *was* a sad story, Jan."

"Yes, but it's *not* anymore. The ending is different."

"What changed?"

"For years I tried everything to heal myself. I wrote and asked why they dismissed me, but all I learned in return was that they thought I lacked a religious disposition because I was gay."

"Well, you *were* gay."

"Yes, but that has nothing to do with a religious disposition, so instead of helping me heal, that information only made it worse."

"What did you do next?

"Well, after years of therapy, anger, grief, and alcohol and drug abuse, I went to the sister who was Provincial Director of the community when I was dismissed. I asked her if she'd let me sit with her and tell my side of the story to her. It was my last ditch effort. Thankfully she accepted and we made a date to get together. I told her the whole story, from age 12 when I decided to be a nun, to the night I was asked to leave and the years after when I went to the mailbox every day hoping for a letter saying they'd made a terrible mistake."

"What did she do?"

"At the end of my story, she asked me to forgive her for the injustice that was done to me under her watch."

"Oh my God...Then what?"

"I forgave her, and then she asked me to forgive the entire congregation for the injustice they did to me as a community."

"Did you?"

"Yes, and then the most amazing thing happened. The whole cloud lifted. It occurred to me that there was nothing to forgive. They had given me the privilege of living a monastic life for two years, of discovering the formula for bliss, of spending an entire year in training for vows, learning how to balance my life with solitude, community, prayer and service. Then they set me free. There was no sad story anymore."

"So what did the story become?"

"A story of nothing to forgive. Of life happening *for* me, not *to* me. A story of gratitude for those two years. where I found my three heroes: the monk Thomas Merton, the activist Dietrich Bonhoeffer, and the mystic/scientist Pierre Teilhard de Chardin. The whole sad story turned into a blessing. It became a power story, just like yours, once I got it straight "

"Wow," she said. "Nice work. Good story!"

"And it only took 20 years," I said, as we both erupted into laughter.

It doesn't matter how long it takes to master our ordeals. It could be decades, with plenty of help from therapists, yoga teachers, spiritual directors, and best friends. That's what we do for each other. We are sounding boards and satellite dishes, listening each other into being, helping each other share and shape the story of our lives.

When Ruth and I make our annual five day photo pilgrimage, a huge number of stories get birthed on the ride from place to place. It's as if our vehicle were a nursery for story seedlings. As we share the events of our lives, they are simultaneously cultivated, fertilized, weeded, pruned. In all the hours that pass from one photo shoot to another, no time is wasted, for we are feverishly unearthing experiences and transforming them into stories.

"So what did it feel like to be a latch-key kid?"

"What's it like to have 65 first cousins and a family reunion every year?"

"Was it scary growing up in south Central L.A?

"Did the sixties turn you into an activist?"

"What does it mean when you say you practice atheism?"

We probe the depths of every subject through the lens of our personal experience, and because we're as different as day and night, the value of our sharing is immeasurable. In *The World is Made of Stories,* David Loy writes: "During their Babylonian exile the Israelites arranged their most cherished stories into the Torah. Celebrating those narratives together kept them a people."[4] Though Ruth and I are only two individuals, the sharing of our stories makes us a people, a tribe, a family. We are bonded by our revelations.

As Joan Didion says, "We tell ourselves stories in order to live." We take the events of our lives, embellish them with juicy details, and spill them like jewels over all our friends. If we do this without mindfulness, forgetful of the energy and power our stories carry, we could find ourselves lost in victim-mode, telling our poor-me stories to conjure up sympathy wherever we can. But what is the value in this?

In an interview in *Common Boundary* magazine, Alice Walker said, "The process of the storytelling is itself a healing process, partly because you have someone there who is taking the time to tell you a story that has great meaning to them. They're taking the time to do this because your life could use some help, but they don't want to come over and just give advice. They want to give it to you in a form that becomes inseparable from your whole self. That's what stories do. Stories differ from advice in that, once you get them, they become a fabric of your whole soul. That is why they heal you." [5]

Twenty years ago, in 1996, Sister Janet Harris, a nun who served as chaplain of LA's Juvenile Hall, started Inside OUT Writers (IOW) with *Los Angeles Times* journalist Duane Noriyuki, and several other professional writers who volunteered to teach creative writing to youth incarcerated in Los Angeles County's Central Juvenile Hall. Their hope was to provide an environment of trust and camaraderie where the students' creativity would be encouraged in spite of the oppressive conditions of detention. What began as three weekly classes has blossomed into 40 classes a week that engage the imaginations of 1800 students per year,

Mindy Velasco, Writing Program Director for IOW said it's difficult to get accurate statistics due to the small sample sizes, but their Alumni program definitely points to a lower rate of recidivism among youth who have been involved in the program.[6] "We limit our classes to 12 students so we can guarantee a feeling of safety and sacred space," said Velasco. "What makes this program so successful is that kids get to share their stories and truths out loud. They are writing as a catharsis, and through their sharing, they begin to see they are not as alone as they thought they were. The sense of community is incredible."

As a complement to the writing classes, IOW also convenes annual Writers' Retreats at each juvenile detention facility and publishes *In Depth,* a quarterly literary journal of students and alumni writings. Since 1996, more than 11,000 youth have participated in over 15,000 classes. In 2009, IOW expanded its work to include efforts to support former students upon their release from detention. The Alumni Program provides a continuum of care to Writing Program students who have been released from detention. They support students with the skills and knowledge necessary to be self-sufficient agents of change in their communities. The Alumni Program has served more than 100 young people and has partnered with over 125 local community organizations to provide dynamic programming and services to meet their needs.

If this can be done in Los Angeles, it can be done anywhere, by any small group of committed people. Everyone has stories. Everyone wants to be heard. As modern day luminary Alan Kay, co-founder of Xerox

PARC says, "Scratch the surface in a typical boardroom and we're all just cavemen with briefcases, hungry for a wise person to tell us stories." But they have to be *good* stories. *Finished* stories. Stories with a conflict, a narrative arc, a resolution, a point. I learned from a couple great mistakes what *doesn't* work.

In 1975, I rode a Honda 400cc motorcycle from Syracuse, New York to California. Originally, I was headed due west, but by the time I got to Rochester, the weather took a turn toward winter. I changed directions and headed south. Hurricane Gladys and I arrived in Florida on the same day. Too exhausted to outrun her, I tented one night on a beach in the panhandle. It was horrific.

Raindrops the size of quarters pelted the tent all night long. Rivers of water streamed in from the sand below, drenching everything in my backpack as I clung to the tent flaps to keep the whole thing from blowing away. The entire night was a battle, and by dawn, every muscle in my body trembled with exhaustion. After three hours in the local laundromat, I loaded up, headed for New Orleans, rode through streets with water up to my knees, and never looked back.

Three weeks later, I landed in Newport Beach, California, feeling like a hero. Surely I could sell my story to *Motorcycle Digest*. I looked up the guidelines, sent them a query letter, and never heard back. I didn't realize until years later why not. It's because I didn't have the story straight. Girl goes across country on a motorcycle is no story. I needed to pitch the conflict, the drama, the resolution. I needed to give them images to see the story as I wanted to tell it. But I didn't.

I signed up for my first writing class a few weeks later. I had to learn the skills. I thought I needed the right words. I didn't even know what the story was. I only knew that I had experienced a big adventure. I tried, in my class, to craft interesting sentences. I tried to be humorous. I used the thesaurus a lot. But I never knew what the story was, so I failed to get published. As E.M. Forster once put it: "The *fact* is the queen died and the king died. The *story* is the queen died and king died of broken heart."

Ten years later, I still hadn't figured it out that every good story requires a dramatic event. The hero has to undergo something that causes a deep change. Conflict is necessary for change to occur.

From 1984-85, I made a one-woman peace pilgrimage around the world. I'd saved $5000 and went as far as I could for as long as I could until my money ran out. I stayed with people in their homes, showed my slideshows of the peace movement and women's movement to whomever I could, and went through 13 countries in 14 months. When I returned, my Uncle Roger arranged a lunch with a journalist friend of his at the Fairmont Hotel in San Francisco. Roger was thrilled that I had accomplished such a feat and was sure the journalist would lead me to the right magazine or newspaper to get the story published.

"So what happened?" the writer asked as soon as he sat down.

"I made a journey for peace around the world," I said.

"Yeah, but what HAPPENED?" he asked again.

He was waiting for the juice, the details. He wanted to know what the battle was, who won, who changed in the end. And I had no idea. I had not harvested my own story yet. I sat there with my mouth open, naïve and voiceless. I hadn't processed it, written it, told it or even understood it as a story of transformation.

Girl makes peace journey around the world is no story. But there *was* a story in there: a story of how a non-religious social activist from the West was unwittingly transformed into a spiritual contemplative by the people who took her in every night on her journey. Every event had its own drama, its own conflict. Every situation with Buddhist, Shinto, Marxist, Communist, Israeli, Palestinian, Hindu, Muslim and Sikh families opened my eyes, challenged my certainties, and opened me up to new ways of thinking and being.

In order to find out what had happened to me, in order to harvest the experience and see what it gave me, I had to externalize it, get it *out* of me. I had to write it down. So I started, country by country, integrating my journal entries, my memories, my photos, letters I had written to friends. Japan, China, Hong Kong, Nepal, the Philippines, Thailand,

India, Israel—into and out of each country over the year long period…
and finally I had a story worth telling. I had a book and I found a publisher who wanted it.

I had to *make something* of my trip in order to assess its value, and it
was the creative act itself that helped me do it. I didn't write because I
had something to say. I wrote to *find out* what I had to say. I wrote the
words to find my voice. And that is often the case. Creativity leads us to
the gold mine. It is what allows us to crystallize our experience, to tone
the muscles of our imagination that we might come to know how it was
that thing happened, and even more, what it had to *give* us.

I had learned I didn't need to choose between East and West,
Buddhism and Christianity, but I needed to fuse them, to incorporate
them both into my being. I'd learned that even though I was a left-lean-
ing progressive, I still had the programming of an "ugly American," and
was quick to judge other countries from the privileged perspective of
my own. I'd learned that time was NOT money, that might was NOT
right. I'd learned that Christianity was too small for me if it insisted on
everyone having a personal relationship with Jesus. As I started to write,
contradictions poured out of me and gave me a glimpse into newfound
complexities, forged in the conflicts I experienced in each new country.
The hero of this journey had transformed dramatically, and the details
of that drama was the stuff of my stories.

OUTGROWING OUR UPBRINGINGS

Many of us think we don't have a story worth telling because we were
rarely mentored in the craft. Children were supposed to be seen and
not heard. Talking about ourselves was generally discouraged. All the
important stories were already written. The inspired literature of our
civilization was already printed and bound, and who were we to think
we could add to the canon? The prophets were all dead. And young
adults today seem more captivated by the screen they're holding than
the scene that's unfolding. The virtual world holds more interest than

the real world, and cyberspace beats outer space and inner space by a long shot. But let's imagine it happening another way.

Imagine that you were born into a time and culture where your human adventures were looked upon as monumental events. Suppose your life was viewed as your classroom, and your homework each night was to review what happened and figure out the lessons you learned. Every day, your teacher would ask what had happened the day before and you would reveal to the class the hope you started out with, the obstacles you encountered, the battle that ensued, and the results. You would wrap it up by saying, "I did a good job and this is what I learned."

If that were the case, not only would you become an expert in mindfulness, carefully observing the present moment as it passed by, but you would also become a quintessential storyteller, having learned through telling and listening the important parts of every good story.

Just as Michelango chiseled his marble into the stunning David, or Virginia Woolf wove her sensibilities and anxieties into her iconoclastic novels, so do we take our raw materials and conjure them into stories that define us. Based on the kind of stories you tell, people will love to see you coming, or not. And this is not to say we will not need assistance in working through our struggles. It is not to undermine the importance of therapeutic work on the heels of devastating experience. Having a witness to our story is often an essential part of healing and transforming it.

In order to recover our well-being, it helps to receive validation from a listener who can receive our pain. That helps us to work through rather than act out whatever emotions are triggered by the event. That was the role the nun who listened to my story played for me. She received my pain so I could finally let it go, knowing I wasn't alone in it. And now I have a story of transformation rather than a poor me story. The process of mining our experiences and turning them into stories that we can offer to others is a process of awakening. As the philosopher Søren Kierkegaard believed: "Only by investing and speaking your vision with passion can the truth, one way or the other, finally penetrate the reluctance of the world".

THE POSITIVE BALANCE OF STORYTELLING

As much as we work our stories, our stories work us. "After stories animate, they instigate," writes Arthur Frank in *The Wounded Storyteller.* Stories can stay with us, haunt us, bring us down, depress our energies, until we come into the awareness that the difficult events of our lives, as much as they took something from us, also gave something to us. We will have fully harvested them when we can acknowledge the reality of both. Yes, there was loss; yes, there was gain.

As storytellers, in mining our experience, we see what it meant to bring us, imagine beyond our emotions into the reasons it might have occurred, the lessons it might be bearing. In an epic sense, we could perceive it as an experience our soul invited, an event that happened to bring us wisdom. To do this, we must leave behind our puny, self-centered thoughts, abandon our desire for pity and sympathy. We must see our lives with new eyes, as adventures we ourselves create with our words, our thoughts, our daily choices. We must see our lives as canvases that we work on all day long, our ongoing masterpieces, the evidence that we were here, and mattered somehow.

The artist Wassily Kandinsky writes in *Concerning the Spiritual In Art* that "the artist must search deeply into his own soul, develop and tend it, so that his art has something to clothe, and does not remain a glove without a hand...*The artist must have something to say,* for mastery over form is not his goal but rather the adapting of form to its inner meaning."

To give our creations or our stories something to clothe, we must have a sense from the outset what they are about. Not to know what the final piece will look like, but to know at the beginning what it means to convey—to have tasted it already in our throats, heard its roar, felt the beat of it in our own hearts. To get our own story straight, we must know what the crisis was, what the hero was after, what rose up as obstacles that needed to be defeated, what was the final resolution? In one lifetime, we will acquire a myriad of stories.

We walk through the minefield every day. Every day we begin with a purpose. Something attempts to thwart us. We turn this way and not that. We win some. We lose some. The point is: we have experienced an adventure, gained a story, and our job, as a creator, is to shape it, color it, breathe life into it, find the treasure in it, so when we tell it to others, they feel the heartbeat of it. It is an intimate act, to create and share these truth nuggets, but it leads to what we are all longing for: being seen and heard on a soulful level.

In *The Life Of Poetry*, Muriel Rukeyser writes that "a work of art is one through which the consciousness of the artist is able to give its emotions to anyone who is prepared to receive them." As one deliberates over the choice of colors in a painting, chords in a musical composition, words in a story, one is reckoning with the emotions that each evokes, attempting to get the outer work as true to the inner feeling as possible. There is a reason an artist chooses cerulean blue over ultramarine or the more passionate vermilion over alizarin crimson. There is a reason why Dixieland jazz is written in major keys and why Moonlight Sonata is minor. There are moods, nuances, subtleties to convey that underline whatever might be called the content of the work and these fine distinctions are what every creative person deals with constantly in the development of her or his work.

In her book, *What Is Found There*, poet Adrienne Rich gives voice to several artists addressing the questions of form, content, and purpose in their work. Sculptor and printmaker Elizabeth Catlett writes, "I learned that my sculpture and my prints had to be based on the needs of people. These needs determine what I do. Some artists say they express themselves: they just reflect their environment. We all live in a given moment in history and what we do reflects what level we are on at that moment. You must, as an artist consciously determine where your own level is."

All of us are at different levels when it comes to creativity. Sometimes we just create because it feels good to be lost in the present moment, and creativity ensures that. Sometimes we create to make something for our loved ones, or as a form of activism, hoping to change consciousness or a cultural mindset. Sometimes we create to escape depression or anxiety. And it never matters where we are at the time or why we're doing what we're doing. On the one hand, it's nobody's business.

And on the other hand, it's possible that the more mindful we are of the many dimensions being brought to the work, the more powerful and illuminated the work itself can become. Poet and painter Michele Gibbs suggests we ask ourselves the following questions as we set out on a creative journey:

1) what are you calling attention to?
2) what energy or action does your creation feed?
3) what reach will your creations have and where are you directing their force?
4) what counts for connection?

The issue of connection here, according to Rich, "implies the centrality of communality in the artistic process." What I put out there in the world, once received by you, has some impact on what you, in turn, put out there in the world. As Nancy Mairs writes in *Voice Lessons*, "Our stories utter one another...If I do my job, the books I write vanish before your eyes. I invite you into the house of my past, and the threshold you cross leads you into your own."

A sculptor friend of mine once said that the work itself is not complete until it is received by the audience, experienced by the viewer. In her opinion, the relationship of viewer to the art is as critical as creator to the art. Each creator forms her own opinion in this matter and there is no one interpretation that is correct, but there is certainly some truth to the assertion that our creations have an impact on each other and can cause change on many levels.

We may or may not remember this as we begin our work, but artists who create with this in mind have a great deal to contribute to the well-being of the human family. No matter what the specific substance of our work, if we approach it with an intention of usefulness beyond self-expression, then we breathe into it an air of universality, a chance that it will matter to more than ourselves that the piece was shaped, the spirit released.

Our task as creators and story-tellers is not to respond to the clamor and demand of contemporary public passions, but to feel for what is missing and bring something to the emptiness. Our challenge is not to look across the landscape of the human experience, but to burrow down into it until we feel the least common denominator that binds us as humans, one to another. Stories and creations that arise from this place do more than mirror the signs of our times. They are more than an echo of what is already sounding. Stories that blend inner knowing with outer experience are fertile and carry with them a prophetic strength: the ability to be not merely a child of the present but a mother of the future. They can carry us forward, teach us, move us to action, change the direction of thought and feeling. These creations carry not just beauty, but the promise of something new.

National Public Radio (NPR) has invited anyone who wants to contribute an essay called *This I Believe* to their ongoing archives of American stories. Fifty-five years ago, people sat by their radios and listened to the voices of politicians, cab drivers, baseball players, and secretaries tell the stories about the core values that guide their daily lives. Today, those essays are still accessible, along with many more. From Albert Einstein to Jackie Robinson, Helen Keller to Helen Hayes, Newt Gingrich to William Buckley to Gloria Steinem, we can read their words and listen to the stories of the well-known and lesser known.

And to guide the writer who wants to contribute, NPR has published some suggestions about telling a story right on their website. "Be specific. Take your belief out of the ether and ground it in the events of your life. Consider moments when belief was formed or tested or changed. Think of your own experience, work and family, and tell of the things you know that no one else does...Make your essay about you; speak in the first person...edit it and simplify until you find the words, tone and story that truly echo your belief and the way you speak."[27]

These are great guidelines for all of us as we wind our way inward, picking up the treasures. They're all there, in our own depths, waiting to be shaped into story, waiting for us to sit down with another and just "go first." At first it is just your words surfacing as the events in your life enfold. You aren't even recognizing them as stories that make up who you are and where you have been. They are just thoughts that help you process where you are in life and what is happening to you. As you mature, you have a larger collection of personal stories.

StoryCorps is a national project that any one of us can work with to record our stories. Since its beginning in 2003 with the opening of a StoryBooth in Grand Central Terminal in New York, Story Corps has been gathering and archiving stories of people from around the country to "remind one another of our shared humanity, to strengthen and build the connections between people, to teach the value of listening, and to weave into the fabric of our culture the understanding that everyone's story matters."[8]

Close to 100 employees serve the organization, collecting stories from everyday people in recording booths in Brooklyn, Chicago, Atlanta and San Francisco. A mobile booth travels across the country recording stories and now there is a free StoryCorps app that anyone can use anywhere.[9]

The app walks users through an interview by providing all the necessary tools: help preparing questions, finding the right environment for your conversation, recording a high-quality interview on your mobile device, sharing the finished product with friends and family, and uploading your conversation to the StoryCorps.me website. You can download it from iTunes or Google Play.

StoryCorps works to include and amplify the voices of people who have been marginalized by society, misrepresented in mainstream media, and excluded from the historical record. A visit to their website will show the many unique initiatives they've taken to ensure this, including the September 11th Initiative, StoryCorpsOutLoud, for the GLBTQ community, StoryCorps Histortias, Memory Loss Initiative, Military Voices Initiative, StoryCorps Griot, and others.

Surfacing and sharing the stories of our lives is a life-changing experience. It alters us. It alters the listeners. It alters the culture. David Loy writes about the power of stories:

Stories justify social distinctions. Medieval kings ruled by divine right; a Rg Veda myth about various parts of Brahma's body rationalizes the Hindu caste system. We challenge a social arrangement by questioning the story that validates it. When people stop believing the stories that justify the social order, it begins to change.[10]

In my work with women with cancer, many survivors have shared the story of cancer's impact on their lives. The stories often reveal a dramatic change that goes beyond anything medical. Many admit that the diagnosis gave them a chance to re-examine what was important in their lives. It stopped them in their tracks and focused their attention on their *own* lives. It allowed them to see how much of their time and energy had gone into taking care of everyone else. It was the wake-up call that changed everything.

In Vermont, at one workshop, a woman introduced herself by saying she had been diagnosed four years ago and given less than a year to live. She was thin, but she looked radiant, vibrant and full of joy. I asked why she thought she was doing so well, what had changed for her after the diagnosis. She said with a big smile, "The day they told me I was dying, I started to really live. I started working part-time. I started yoga. I took painting lessons and voice lessons. And I buy all the books and music I want to buy." Her entire story changed, and her telling it changed the rest of us in the room. It made us rethink our own choices, re-examine our relationship to time, to our creativity, to our health.

As Christina Baldwin writes in *Story Catcher,* "Story is the electromagnetic conductor that brings us close enough together to make the leap of association and identification, to see that another person is a variation of ourselves. We are in grave danger if we lose our link to our own stories." Magic happened that night in Vermont and it happened because of one woman's story and her willingness to share it. She helped us to see ourselves as variations of her. And that made all the difference.

In my room that night, I opened my copy of Steven Pressfield's *War of Art*. I read the passage: "The part of us that we imagine needs healing is not the part we create from; that part is far deeper and stronger. The part we create from can't be touched by anything our parents did, or society did. That part is unsullied, uncorrupted, soundproof, weatherproof, bulletproof. In fact, the more troubles we've got, the better and richer that part becomes."

Amen, I thought. So be it.

CHAPTER 8

BELIEVING IS SEEING: WHY YOUR LIFE IS TURNING OUT LIKE IT IS

*Things behave in alignment with how the observer expects them
to behave, so as we change our collective story about the state of
the world the state of the world also changes.*
ARJUNA ARDAGH

PUSHING OURSELVES TOWARD CLARITY

MANY OF US were led to believe that life is happening to us, that there
is some Heavenly Being pulling all the strings and we are like pup-
pets reacting to the dramas being initiated by God, or Fate, or "the
Universe." We sing "He's Got the Whole World In His Hands" like we
have no responsibility for how life is unfolding on the planet. I heard a
Congressman on C-span say it was blasphemous for us to worry about
global climate change because it's in the hands of God and none of our
business.

A few years ago, I had an experience that turned my thinking around
in the matter of God and creativity. I was carpooling in an RV with
two women from San Diego, heading for Santa Fe, New Mexico where I
was leading a workshop. Halfway there, my artist friend Jane announces
she's an atheist.

"Jane," I say, "You're going to a workshop called *Divining the Body.*
You're going to be the only atheist in the room."

"That's ok. I usually am."

"What do you do when everybody talks about God like they do?"

"Oh, I'm used to it now. You can forget about it. It won't matter."

But I couldn't forget about it. I drove hundreds of miles pondering how I could make this feel as good for Jane at it was going to feel for everyone else. I didn't want her to feel excluded. I didn't want to use a language that was foreign to her. My job as a facilitator is to create a sense of oneness, and I had my work cut out for me. I could see that.

We stopped at the Albuquerque airport to pick up three women from Missouri who started talking about God the moment they arrived. God did this. God did that. Every time I heard the word, my ears burned.

"It was raining, but God got us a great taxi-driver who got us there on time."

"I was married to an alcoholic, but God set it up that way so I'd learn patience.

"God helped me find just the right man on e-harmony…God gave me a child with disabilities…God gave me cancer because…"

Every time I heard the word God, I wanted to say "Who exactly are you talking about and how does this work?"

We pulled into the retreat center parking lot and had two hours before our first gathering. I still had no idea how to handle things, but a thought occurred to me as I entered our meeting room. We sat in a circle and I said to the group, "There's only one rule for the entire weekend. You can share anything you want, but you can't used the word 'GOD.'"

"Why not?" came a few voices from around the circle.

"Because we're trying an experiment. We're trying to take things to a deeper level here, trying to speak as clearly and concretely as we can. If we have to come up with new ways to describe what we're talking about, we'll push ourselves toward more clarity because we won't be able to fall back on a conceptual word that might not work for everyone in the group. It's a global world now and we have to practice speaking and relating to people who don't necessarily share our notion of God."

They agreed and we kept the rule all weekend. People slipped up right and left, "God this, God that…all during the introductions, but by

Saturday, they had retrained their brains and the energy changed dramatically. They were beginning to speak from their own power centers. By Sunday lunchtime, an incredible power surged through our group. Women were grounded in their speaking. Their words radiated with self-authority. They claimed their wisdom, shared their journeys, and took responsibility for the lives they had created. Though it didn't come naturally in the early stages, by the end of the weekend they were pros in sharing their essences.

No one had to point to the heavens, abdicate their power, give credit or blame to the Heavenly Father. Instead they praised themselves, acknowledged their courage, and shared the stories of what they had accomplished. David Bohm writes in *On Dialogue* that to communicate means "to make something common." And that's what we did. We made of our language a common language that transcended all barriers. As a result, our spirituality was fortified that weekend—deepened, to a large extent, for most of the women.

And all because one woman admitted to being a non-believer, just as a matter of self-disclosure. She did not share it to change things, to have me rearrange the program. It was simply her way of being authentic with me. And as a result, all heaven broke loose. It was our diversity that led to our change of language, which in turn led to our self-referential speaking. And because of the power of every woman's speaking, the collective resonance in the group built up strength.

Because of our commitment to stay on common ground, the intensity of our light shifted from incandescent to laser. In ordinary light, the light waves go in all different directions and the patterns are incoherent. In laser light, the waves all go in one direction and a great power comes from that coherence. Our group was laser-like in its clarity because our language was rooted in the concrete, grounded in the finite world. Its lack of reference to anything conceptual or abstract is the very thing that made our words so muscular and hardy. Like the difference between a Hallmark card and a Mary Oliver poem—it's all in the concrete details.

Since that retreat I have made it a practice to avoid using the word God. I see why Meister Eckhart said that the process of enlightenment is a process of subtraction, not addition. Eckhart believed that we have to leave the *concept* of God to have an *experience* of God, and that is just what I saw happening in Santa Fe. As women changed their language about a God who is making everything happen, they started to refer to themselves as agents in the matter. They started to talk as if they, too, were creating the reality they were entering into. And this is just what science is showing these days through a number of experiments: *reality begins with our thoughts.*

Long before physicists studied the science of consciousness in laboratories, metaphysicians were marrying ideas from ancient sages with their own spiritual experiences and uncovering the role of mind in the making of matter. In his classic book, *Thoughts Are Things*, Ernest Holmes reveals his ideas about the power of our thoughts. "The images of your thought attract to you circumstances and situations which are like them. It is the nature of thought to externalize itself, bringing about conditions which exactly correspond to the thought...Every thought is in some respect a prayer, a creative factor in our experience...The future always does take care of itself, but it is born out of what you are thinking today."[1]

CREATING REALITY

To get what you want, you have to see it, think about it, focus on it. If you focus on your fears, it only makes sense they will be activated. If you think only of your heart's desire, then that will be the reality that becomes your life. Thoughts draw like things to themselves, so have loving, positive, abundant, creative thoughts and see what you attract.

Jane Roberts has written a series of consciousness-related books where she channels a discarnate entity known as Seth. While Seth's language is not as accessible as Holmes,' they say basically the same thing. I have read several of the Seth books, which I consider an ultimate creative collaboration. They have stimulated my imagination, altered my thoughts, and heightened my ability for self-reflection. These words are from the book, *The Seth Material:*

In your system of reality you are learning what mental energy is, and how to use it. You do this by constantly transforming your thoughts and emotions into physical form. You are supposed to get a clear picture of your inner development by perceiving the exterior environment. What seems to be a perception, an objective concrete event independent from you, is instead the materialization of your own inner emotions, energy, and mental environment.[2]

Physicist William Tiller performed a series of experiments with a team of scientists that illustrate the power of our minds to alter matter. A deep and impenetrable mystery lies at the heart of *how* this works, but the fact that it *does* work is undeniable. In his book, *Conscious Acts of Creation,* Tiller unfolds three scientific experiments with all their formulaic splendor that shows how an Intention-Imprinted Electrical Device (a box into which people have imprinted their conscious intention to cause a change) caused the following events to occur:

1.) increase the pH of water by one full pH unit with no chemical additions;

2.) change the *in vitro* enzymatic and co-enzyme activity in human cells;

3.) enhance the [ATP]/[ADP] ratio in the cells of developing fruit fly larva to shorten larval development times.[3]

Few people will want to wade through the many pages of physics formulae and complex illustrations in his book, but that is not necessary for our point here. We are simply trying to show that there is scientific evidence proving that consciousness and intention have the power to change things in the material world. With our mind alone, we can change matter

Tiller has provided us with a diagram of how this may work in the living of our lives. We're including it here, since a picture is worth a thousand words, and it may help us understand the concept, but even Tiller warns against taking it too literally. He writes, "Any model, no matter how seemingly successful, will eventually be proven incomplete in detail. Its primary purpose is to act as a vehicle which gives a sense of understanding that triggers the proper set of questions or experiments needed to probe deeper." This diagram certainly provokes a whole new set of questions, but it does offer a way of visualizing how this mysterious, word-defying phenomenon occurs.

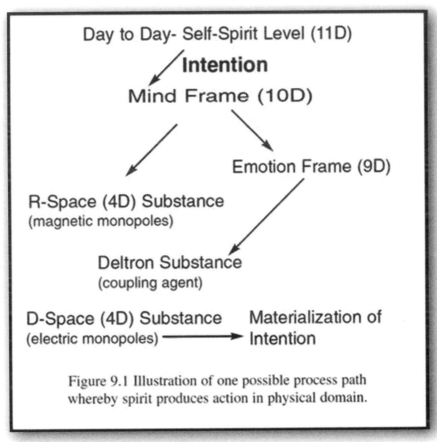

Figure 9.1 Illustration of one possible process path whereby spirit produces action in physical domain.

Illustration from Conscious Acts of Creation. Used with permission of William Tiller, PhD.

To paraphrase Tiller's explanation of how this works:

1. A specific intention, projected from the spirit level, imprints a detailed pattern on the mind. This pattern is an information pattern that represents the original intention.

2. The intention is then imprinted onto the magnetic monopole layer and the emotion domain layer where it activates the coupling substance, deltrons. Deltron particles can interact with etheric particles traveling faster than light and also interact with physical particles traveling slower than light, and can thus bring about energy exchange between them.

3. The deltrons allow coupling between the magnetic monopole and the electric monopole. The deltrons coupling agent acts like the "toner" used in a copy machine to produce a clear copy of something.

4. Once the original imprint has been coupled by the electric and magnetic monopoles, it activates the built-in mechanisms for action in the surrounding domain—physical reality.

To state this in other words, following Tiller's model: Spirit imprints a thought on our mind. It then reaches our emotions and magnetic monopoles, where the coupling agent deltrons gets the electrical field involved, which causes the idea to move forward toward manifest reality. Tiller believes that we respond to the events of our lives via thoughts, attitudes and actions. This feedback allows our mind and emotion domains to make incremental changes to the original imprint patterns.

While it is true that science is not capable of providing us with absolute truth, it can and does provide relative knowledge about relationships between different phenomena. We are not invested in defending Tiller's assertions here as much as we are interested in providing new images and metaphors for understanding our role as conscious creators of *this* life on *this* earth. One need not abandon the notion of a Cosmic Creator, but one must transcend the idea that life is happening *to* us, without our involvement.

To give up that notion is not blasphemous, anymore than giving up Santa or the Tooth Fairy was blasphemous. As we mature, we let go of our childish ideas and step into our role as co-creators. If one believes there is a God, and we are made in God's image, it makes sense that we would follow in the steps of the Creator, co-creating relationships, families, communities and cultures that are based on love, beauty, kindness. The prophet Micah calls for the faithful to "act justly, love mercy and walk humbly with their God."

For those who do not believe in a personal God, there may be no religious mandate, but there is a *human* and moral mandate to tend to the earth, to follow the Golden Rule, to work with others to create safe and peaceful communities. One's religion or lack of religion is a moot point. We are born to create. We are progeny of Creation Itself, manifestations of our planet's desire to be fruitful and multiply.

As caretakers and culture-makers, our handprints are all over everything. The dominant myths and stories of our time are losing their grip on the collective imagination. Rugged individualism is being supplanted by an awareness of our connectedness and interdependence. Few are waiting for saviors and superheroes to rescue us from our ruins. The most evolutionary of leaders are creating new networks and communities wherever they can. Unchecked progress has outgrown its usefulness and we are in search of sustainable pathways to prosperity. The seeds of a new human story are blowing in these winds of change. As David Loy writes, "We need new stories that account for climate change and enable us to address it. We cannot simply un-story global warming, although some fossil fuel companies have tried."[4]

Intelligence-at-Large (or the Cosmos, Creator, Creation) is broadcasting information to us every moment of the day. Thousands of thoughts cross the sky of our mind and we (consciously or not) choose which ones we want to focus on, explore, expand. Because our emotions are involved in the process, we have feelings about certain thoughts. Our desires are awakened. Our imaginations are sparked. And if we are free from disabling thoughts and beliefs that disempower us, we can begin the process of converting our desires into reality. We scatter our wishes every which way until we step into the reality we have put in place through our, intentions, words, and actions. This is called *creating our lives.*

Quantum physicist Amit Goswami speaks of the process in these terms:

> The creative act is the fruit of the encounter of the self's classical and quantum modalities. The classical modality of the self, like the classical computer, deals with information, but the self's quantum modality deals with communication. Thus the first stage of the play of creativity is the tangled play of information (development of expertise) and communication (development of openness). It is tangled because you cannot tell when information ends and communication begins; there is a discontinuity in the "cosmic message." A creative experience is one of the few times when we directly experience the quantum modality with little or no time lag. It is this encounter with primary process experience that produces the elation, the ah-ha, the creative act of self-realization. It can lead directly to personal transformation of one's own context of living.[5]

Goswami uses the diagram you've probably seen a hundred times to illustrate the point. Whatever you choose to focus on—the wife or the mother-in-law-becomes the very thing you see at the present moment. You cannot experience both simultaneously and it is always your choice, your focus, that brings one and not the other to life.

It is a transformative experience to go from being a victim of life to a creator of life. Tons of corrupt software files must be deleted from your brain. Psychologist and physician Dr. Joan Borysenko wrote that "the hardware for omniscience is installed in our brains." Neurologist Candance Pert put it this way: "Blessing and bliss come from the same root. We are hard-wired to be in bliss." Bliss is our natural state, our default mode. But most of us have been programmed since childhood to think just the opposite. *Life is too hard. Bliss is for the enlightened ones who meditate all day. I'm not smart enough or creative enough to make something*

How many figures can you see in the image below?

Answer: If you look closely, you can see both a young
and an elderly woman.
This picture, My Wife and My Mother-in-Law, is a good
example of two images existing in one, and was
published in 1915 by the cartoonist W.E. Hill.

happen. I'll never get it right. *I'm a sinner and I am not worthy.* Hundreds of these deadening illusions fill our brain and keep us silent.

Illusions are false beliefs. They are notions and ideas that we have inherited from our culture, our families, and almost every institution with which we've been associated. Illusions take up residence in our minds because we receive them when we are young, impressionable, trusting, and open to the ideas being handed down to us. They are part of our social conditioning, but they do not serve us. Illusions are, in fact, the only cause of our unhappiness.

The Indian philosopher Sri Aurobindo said, "In order to see, you have to stop being in the middle of the picture." This means we have to step outside of ourselves, put some distance between ourselves and our thoughts, so we can assess their heritage and test them for authenticity. Each of us must do the deep and personal work of tending to our thoughts, since they are the wellspring from which our life bubbles up. We must begin to hear ourselves think, and then hear ourselves speak, as if every thought and sentence were the seeds of our tomorrow.

To do this is a spiritual discipline, a mindfulness practice, a commitment. It is yoga for the soul. Since it's true that we create our lives with our thoughts, words and intentions, it's crucial that we start thinking and talking about what we really want. In our prayers and intentions, we connect our local mind with global mind and express gratitude for whatever it is we imagine coming our way. We are thankful *in advance* for the manifestation of our dream. We are aware that many possibilities come our way from the infinite realm, but that we choose the particular one we wish to experience. Global mind throws a deck of cards our way. We pick a card. That becomes our reality, until we choose another one.

There is a guided meditation online that might help you reflect on and embody these ideas. It is called *Think of Yourself* and the music and images help to bring these intellectual ideas into the heart zone where they can inspire us.[6] I will include the text at the end of this chapter. It is also available as a bonus track on my CD *Ever With You*.

Or you can try this practice, suggested by the Indian neurologist Dr Pankaj Gupta:

Sit comfortably in a chair or on the floor. Imagine a soft ball in your chest. Close your eyes and take this ball to each of your toes and then each part of your body feeling its warmth, all this while breathing slowly but deeply. At the end of one session as you return the ball to your chest, think of an act of kindness such as of giving a blanket to a man shivering in cold. Slowly, after several sessions your mind and body will glow with love and compassion.[7]

WHAT IS BEST FOR THE WHOLE?

A few years ago, I was eating dinner with friends at a small Italian restaurant when three men with guns walked through the door. "Get up!"

they shouted as they approached our table. We were stunned and sat frozen in our seats, none of us moving. Two of them walked through the swinging doors into the kitchen and the other came closer with his gun pointing. "Keep your eyes down and get into the kitchen, now! And take your bags!" By now it had sunk in that this was really happening and we all stood up and headed into the kitchen, the gunman behind us.

"Don't anybody look," he warned. "Just lie down on the floor and keep your eyes shut." We did as he said, and took our places on the floor, along with the kitchen staff, who were already lying face down. He told the men to put their wallets on the floor, then instructed all of us to remove our jewelry and watches and put them on the floor next to our purses. "Keep your eyes shut," he kept shouting while his cohorts collected the wallets and jewelry.

They went into the office next, while one kept guard over us. I heard someone go through the swinging door, and then there was a long silence. I thought they had left, so I lifted up my head and looked toward the door, just as one pushed it open. He saw me looking and came at me with his gun pointed at my head, shouting "I told you to keep your eyes shut!"

Here's my choice point. What am I going to make of this moment?

"I can't see anything without my glasses," I lied, burrowing my head under my arms. Suddenly the strangest thing happened. I saw the whole scene from above, as if I were suspended from the ceiling. As I viewed our bodies sprawled out on the greasy kitchen floor, powerless and terrified, I heard a voice in my head: "This is what we've come to. This is what we're making of our great human opportunity." And out of my right eye, as I lie there, one big tear fell on the floor.

In this moment, my local brain and global mind became one. The local me was the victim, paralyzed with fear, worried for my life, grieving over an image seen by the global me—an image of my own tribe run amok. From that upper view, I was a witness, not a victim. I was the many, not the one—the "we," not the "I."

Now, as I think back on this event, I find that it gave me a metaphor for understanding the distinction between global and local, and seeing that they are two sides of one coin. My reality is simultaneously local and global. I am at once the witness and the witnessed, the creator of experience and the one who experiences it. I am like the cell in the organism—offering my vitality to the whole and taking my vitality from it. A singular and unique entity, I bring to the whole what no one else can bring, and doing that, I find my place in the family of things.

It is at the intersection of local brain and global mind that our creative fire is ignited and fanned. It is here, when these poles are brought together, that original thoughts are conceived and born, that the future enters into us before it happens. It is the recognition of our oneness that causes the quantum leap to a higher level of thinking. Einstein wrote: "The world that we have made as a result of the level of thinking we have done thus far creates problems which cannot be solved by the same level of thinking in which they were created." Until we shift into global mind thinking we cannot solve the problems that we have created with local brain thoughts. As Deepak Chopra says, "Our problems are in the field of diversity. Our solutions are in the field of unity."

We have built a world based on our separation from each other and it is unsustainable. To create a world that is just and sustainable, we must design and build with our oneness in mind, asking ourselves at every point, *What is best for the whole?* When I think of creators, visionaries, leaders, I think of those who draw us after them, whose energy field, like that of a magnet, extends beyond the body itself, attracting others to the brightness of their light. It is true for all of us, that our heart energy precedes us as we navigate through life, extending beyond us as an aura potent enough to affect those in our path—but there is something particularly uplifting about the energy of people who are aware of the threads that connect us all and whose work in the world reflects this knowing. We are strongly affected by each person's energy, as studies in this area are now confirming.

Ruth writes about a time when this became clear:

For ten years straight, my husband and I went to the Golden Door, a week-long spa experience near San Diego, for couples week. The Golden Door was one of the first health and wellness spas in our area. It has acres and acres of wooded oaks and natural chaparral along with mature Japanese Gardens and camellia bushes the size of large trees.

Over the course of ten years, many couples return time after time so we got to know them very well. Some became good friends and traveling companions, and others we saw only once a year but there was a bond that was created among many of us and we were like family for that week.

I had one friend who felt my life had been much more interesting than hers. I asked her why she felt that way as I had gone through experiences that I wouldn't wish on anyone else. My early life had been shaped by chaos, upset, disappointment.

My friend said that her life was like Wonder bread. Nothing unusual or bad or amazing had ever happened to her or her family. She was from the Midwest. She was born into an upper middle-class family, went to the right college, married the right boy, had the right kids, lived in the right home and then she was getting ready to retire in the appropriate retirement environment. She longed for experiences that were challenging, that gave one the opportunity to prove oneself. So she liked to hear my stories of triumph over tragedy.

One of our morning rituals was a 3 ½ mile hike at 5:30 a.m. The terrain was up and down and you had to be in pretty good shape, so the same folks showed up every morning to share a cup of green tea, a morning meditation and speak about the night's activities. This same woman always wanted to walk behind me. We would talk and laugh but much of the trail was only wide enough for one person. And she was always right behind me.

I finally asked her why. She said she loved my energy. She loved watching my macro view of what was around me. She said I looked down almost beneath the surface and found things of interest. She felt my intimacy with nature. She was moved by my love for the Earth and she wanted to understand how I saw, to find what I found.

I explained that the world we see at eye level is easy for me to miss. The things at eye level become commonplace, but when I take a macro look at the smallest things around, I find amazing things. The little tiny leaves are as perfectly formed and complex as the largest of leaves. The bark on a twig is as complex as that of the biggest tree. Little minute flowers on weeds viewed up close have exactly the same complexity and characteristics as a beautiful orchid.

She walked behind me for the whole week and I'll never know the impact of that. I only know that we make a difference to each other, that our energy and actions matter a lot, even in the tiniest ways.

HOW WE MATTER

That we have an effect on others is a matter of fact; the *kind* of effect we have on others is a matter of consciousness. We can radiate blessings and light or negativity and darkness. It is in our best interests to be mindful of our energy as we scatter it about, because thoughts can produce effects only of the same nature. Kindness to others favors a nervous system that is kind to itself, says to the *Bhagavad Gita*. And Joseph Chilton Pearce says it even more clearly in *The Biology of Transcendence*: "Every negative thought I entertain in my head, which I think is my own secret pace, actually strengthens the negative field that sweeps our world. Every time I bemoan the negative world out there that I must suffer, I have supported and contributed to it through my moaning. My secret place in my head is not so secret after all."[8]

This is global mind thinking. It is counterintuitive for some, for we have been trained to think otherwise, but it is the very essence of creative thinking. Before we can manage anything or anyone in the outside world, we must first learn to manage our energy and thoughts, to synchronize our mind and our emotions for optimal performance. Then we will be ready to enter deeper levels of consciousness, increase our intuitive capacities, and tap into a creativity greater than we have ever known.

A study of workers in a high-tech company who took a two month training program in meditation showed a major change in brain activity, declines in anxiety, and beneficial changes in immune function. "Happiness and compassion are skills that can be trained," according to researcher Richard Davidson.[9]

Even without a concerted commitment to meditation, anyone can start a practice of mindfulness that involves two simple steps. This one is suggested by HeartMath and it's called the Quick Coherence technique[10]:

1. Focus your attention in the area of your heart. Imagine your breath is flowing in and out of your heart. Breathe a little slower and deeper than usual. (Inhale five seconds, exhale five seconds, or whatever rhythm is most comfortable for you).

2. Activate a positive feeling. Make a sincere attempt to experience a regenerative feeling such as appreciation or care for someone or something in your life. (Think of a person, an occasion, an accomplishment, maybe a pet—something that gives you a sense of calm or comfort).

    If you use this technique when you begin to feel an anger, anxiety or stress, you can balance your emotions and thoughts and come to a state of clarity. Ultimately, this practice can lead to more balanced heart rhythms, better brain functioning, and more access to higher intelligence.

A creative approach to community meditation was initiated by Jeffrey Zlotnick in San Diego in 2003. Zlotnik, a former corporate consultant, founded the Meditation Initiative and has worked to bring the mental health benefits of mindfulness and meditation to the public for free. He began meditating in 1996, while working at a Group Home for Abused Teens. After noticing tremendous change in their attitudes after meditating, Zlotnick started expanding the program to accommodate more people. Since January of 2009, the Meditation Outreach Program has sat in meditation with more than 25,100 people. The Initiative has led free meditation for Homeless Teens, K-12 Public Schools, Juvenile Detention

Facilities, Federal and State Prisons, Wounded Warriors, Sober Living Homes, Jewish Family Services, Catholic Charities and Group Homes for Victims of Domestic Violence and Human Trafficking, and several other organizations.

A friend of mine, Rande Wegman, is a mindfulness teacher who volunteers for the program. We met yesterday after she facilitated a meditation for hundreds of people in the new San Diego Library. "It was a beautiful occasion," she said. "People from every imaginable station in life sitting together, breathing together, being at peace together. It's so inspiring to be part of." To fund the project, The Initiatiave invites corporate sponsors in the community to pay for the venues. It's a grassroots effort, but one that is leading to a more peaceful environment in San Diego.

In an email he sent to his subscribers this week, Zlotnick writes:

In the last few days alone, Meditation Initiative led free meditations for 40 staff members at Pacific which is a Digital Marketing Agency, 60 staff members at San Diego County Public Authority (In-Home Supportive Services), 12 staff members at San Diego Regional Center which provides services to people with devclopmental disabilities, 5 Wounded Warriors with PTSD at the Naval Medical Center San Diego, 20 Students at Southwestern College as a part of their Health and Wellness Program and 40 Inmates in a local San Diego Prison. This is a pretty typical week for The Meditation Initiative.

Their website states that

"Meditation is not an escape from reality; it is direct perception into your own mind and your own thoughts. When we are in a good mood, it is from thoughts we have, when we are in a bad mood, it is from thoughts we have. Once we stop trying to change everything outside of us and we work on changing our mind and our heart and our reaction to the world around us, life gets a little easier, a little more peaceful, a little happier, yet ultimately nothing changed except our own mind.[11]

THE HEART-BRAIN CONNECTION

When we are born, the DNA in our bodies contains the blueprints for who we are and instructions for who we will become. Researchers at the HeartMath Institute (HMI) say factors such as appreciation and love or anger and anxiety influence and can alter our DNA blueprints. When we are agitated, our energy reserves are redirected from keeping our biological systems in good repair to confronting the stresses created by our negative thoughts and feelings. Our immune systems are compromised by stress.

To explore the relationships between our feelings and our physical well-being, HMI has been performing research for two decades. In one experiment, an individual holding three DNA samples was directed to generate *heart coherence* – a beneficial state of mental, emotional and physical balance and harmony – with the coherence technique mentioned earlier in this chapter. The individual succeeded, as instructed, to intentionally and simultaneously unwind two of the DNA samples to different extents and leave the third unchanged.

The results provide experimental evidence to support the hypothesis that aspects of the DNA molecule can be altered through intentionality. If you think of our DNA as a kind of scroll, you can see the advantage of having the strands relax and unwind. Just as we can access more information from a scroll that is unwound, so can the body access more information from DNA strands that are unwound. Anger tightens DNA strands. Appreciation unwinds them. Thought management matters significantly.

While persons capable of generating high ratios of heart coherence were able to alter DNA according to their intentions, control group participants who showed low ratios of heart coherence were not able to achieve such results.[12] These studies are pointing to the connections between mindfulness and well-being. It is no longer just a metaphysical assertion that our thoughts become our reality.

In another HMI study, leukocytes (white blood cells) were harvested for DNA and placed in chambers to be measured for electrical charges.

The donor, who sat in another room, was subjected to emotional stimulation, such as war images, sexual erotica, and humor. When the donor exhibited emotional peaks and valleys, measured by electrical responses, so did the DNA *at same time*. This was also true when researchers separated the donor by fifty miles. It is a non-local, sub-atomic, quantum reality. Our DNA is affected by our emotions.

Another study showed that when people touch or are in close proximity, one person's heartbeat signal is registered in the other person's brain waves. More refined techniques have since been developed that indicate there is an energy exchange that occurs up to five feet away from the body even without touching. Because the changes in DNA in these experiments actually occur biologically in a number of vital cell functions, including DNA replication and repair, the concept that human intention can influence processes in human cells is supported. The finding that heart coherence was key in achieving the results of these experiments may lead to a better understanding of the role of positive feelings and attitudes in these critical areas: health and healing; phenomena such as the placebo effect; spontaneous remission in cancer; and the positive effects of prayer.[13]

The heart is a sophisticated information processing center with its own nervous system. Its electrical field is 100 times stronger than the brain and its magnetic field is 5000 times stronger than the brain. It has the ability to sense, learn, remember, and make functional decisions independent of the brain. It sends messages to the brain and the rest of the body in four different languages—neurological, bio-physical, hormonal, and electrical—and these messages cause our awareness to expand.

Conclusions that the heart receives and responds to intuitive information were based on a study where thirty calm and fifteen emotionally arousing pictures were presented to 26 participants. Measurements included skin conductance; the electroencephalogram (EEG), to measure electrical activity changes in the brain; and the electrocardiogram (ECG), to measure electrical activity changes in the heart. These measures were used to investigate where and when in the brain and body intuitive information is processed. The results showed that the heart appears to receive and respond to intuitive information before communicating that information to the brain. They also found significant gender differences in the processing of prestimulus information. Females, it turns out, are more attuned to intuitive information from the heart. Women's intuition is a real thing. What we learn from this study is that the body's perceptual apparatus is constantly scanning the future.[14] Our bodies actually sense the future before it arrives.

Rainer Maria Rilke spoke of this in his book *Letters to a Young Poet:*

It seems to me that almost all our sadnesses are moments of tension, which we feel as paralysis because we no longer hear our astonished emotions living. Because we are alone with the unfamiliar presence that has entered us; because everything we trust and are used to is for a moment taken away from us; because we stand in the midst of a transition where we cannot remain standing. That is why the sadness passes: the new presence inside us, the presence that has been added, has entered our heart, has gone into its innermost chamber and is no longer even there, is already in our bloodstream. And we don't know what it was. We could easily be made to believe that nothing happened, and yet we have changed, as a house that a guest has entered changes.

We can't say who has come, perhaps we will never know, but many signs indicate *that the future enters us in this way in order to be transformed in us, long before it happens.* And that is why it is so important to be solitary and attentive when one is sad: because the seemingly uneventful and motionless moment when our future steps into us is so much closer to life than that other loud and accidental point of time when it happens to us as if from outside. The quieter we are, the more patient and open we are in our sadnesses, the more deeply and serenely the new presence can enter us, and the more we can make it our own, the more it becomes our fate; and later on, when it "happens" (that is, steps forth out of us to other people), we will feel related and close to it in our innermost being…

So you mustn't be frightened, dear Mr. Kappus, if a sadness rises in front of you, larger than any you have ever seen; if an anxiety, like light and cloud-shadows, moves over your hands and over everything you do. You must realize that something is happening to you, that life has not forgotten you, that it holds you in its hand and will not let you fall.[15]

Because our bodies are scanning the future constantly, we are experiencing in our cells and in our consciousness feelings and perceptions that we've never had before. Though we have no words for it, we are coming to understand more deeply the meaning of *oneness*. As Susan Griffin writes, " At the center of all my sorrows, I have felt a presence that was not mine alone." It sends shivers up the spine to read the Hassidic saying, *When the ax enters the forest, the trees, upon seeing its wooden handle, say "Look, one of us."* It's chilling to read the Nigerian tribal chief's warning: "If you do not share your wealth with us, we will share our poverty with you."

Coherence is the synchronization of mind and heart—intellect and emotion—allowing us to find clarity in the midst of chaos. At the global level, coherence is the synthesis of all the parts into one harmonious whole. It is what enables us to choose wisely, to think strategically, to manage our feelings, to communicate effectively, to lead people, and to be more attuned to the needs of others. When our hearts and minds are in harmony, we have more power, more insight, more courage. As Joseph Chilton Pearce puts it in *Biology of Transcendence*, "An unconflicted person has dominion over a conflicted or divided person."

We are living in a moment of accelerated collective fear because of the rise of terrorism around the world. Fear, because it throws us into an ancient survival mentality, shuts down our higher modes of evolutionary awareness. Our ability to think creatively is compromised by the stress that such fear and anxiety cause. It is only through mindfulness that we can pull ourselves back from the fray and shift into a higher mode of functioning. When we are conscious of our thoughts, disavow fear and come into heart-brain coherence, we simultaneously draw upon our heart's intelligence, defuse the defensive circuit, and engage the creative forebrain. This breaks the bonds of ancient instinctual behavior and opens us to the possibility of transcendence. This is what it means to rewire our neural networks. It happens one conscious thought at a time.

"That we are shaped by the culture we create makes it difficult to see that our culture is what must be transcended, which means we must rise above our notions and techniques of survival itself, if we are to survive," writes Pearce. It means, first of all, that we must rise above our notions of separateness and powerlessness, and open our eyes to all the evidence that proves otherwise. It means we need to consider, as Matthew Fox once suggested, *outlawing war as we once outlawed slavery*. It means we need to achieve coherence within ourselves so we have the insight and intuition necessary to create new structures as the old ones crumble.

When the Nobel Prize winner, chemist Ilya Prirogine, spoke about systems evolving, he said that as long as a system is stable, you can't change it, but as it moves toward disequilibrium and falls into chaos, the slightest bit of coherent energy can bring it into a new structure. Those of us who are consciously creating, who are giving voice to our visions and taking a stand for a sustainable world, we *are* that coherent energy that is attracting the new into existence. Only this time, what we are creating is not based on Newtonian science which claims that the universe is one of independent, separate entities, but on quantum science which sees the universe as a process: a changing, flowing, evolving, and intimately interconnected system of interactions.

WHERE GLOBAL CONSCIOUSNESS MIGHT TAKE US

Even robots have been documented responding to the power of thought. Eighty different groups were tested in one experiment involving a robot programmed for random movement and baby chicks. The robot was sent into a room full of baby chicks in bright daylight, and its movements were all observed to be random in nature. Knowing that the chicks prefer well-lit rooms, the researchers then devised an experiment where they turned off all the lights, leaving the chicks in the dark. The chicks became afraid and huddled together in the corner. The experimenters then sent in a robot carrying a lighted candle. In 71 percent of the cases, the robot spent excessive time in the vicinity of the chicks. Its former random movements were now overpowered by the *desire* of the chicks for its light.[16] There is mind in all matter and the power of our desire can influence it. If a group of chicks can overpower the movements of a robot programmed for randomness, just think what you can achieve with the power of your desire.

Physicist Max Planck wrote, "All matter originates and exists only by virtue of a force which brings the particles of an atom to vibration and holds this most minute solar system of the atom together...We must assume behind this force the existence of a conscious and intelligent mind. This mind is the matrix of all matter." The *who* that we are is one with this matrix. We are the vessels through which it operates, as the light bulb is a vessel for electricity. The force comes through us, taking whatever shape we give it. Whether one is a terrorist or a piano tuner, a murderer or a mystic, the very same force is behind each individual, holding the atoms and cells together, unifying us in the web of existence.

When Einstein reached the conclusion that "something deeply hidden had to be behind things," it is this force he was talking about. When the Indian mystic Sri Aurobindo wrote, "That within us which seeks to know and to progress is not in the mind but something behind it which makes use of it," he, too, was referring to the Consciousness of which we are a part and to whom we belong.

In his book *The Great Work*, cultural historian and visionary ecologist Thomas Berry writes:

We must consciously will the further stages of evolutionary process. Our responsibility is to be present to the Earth in its next sequence of transformations. While we were unknowingly carried through the evo-lutionary process in former centuries, the time has come when we must in some sense guide and energize the process ourselves[17]

Two current examples of this come to mind. In a recent New York Times Magazine article, a story was told of an artist, Rick Lowe, who sought to address in his paintings the violence and poverty he witnessed all around him in the black communities of Houston.[18] In 1990, when a group of high school students visited Lowe's studio, one young man asked him, rather than making work about the difficult, daily reality of the Third Ward residents, why he didn't try to *affect* that reality.

That question sparked an evolution, not only in Lowe's thinking and artmaking, but also in the work of two fellow artists, Theaster Gates and Mark Bradford. As they started to think more expansively about their work, they each questioned the purpose of it, how it should be seen and even where it should live.

Within two years, Lowe, in collaboration with several other artists, purchased 22 abandoned tenant farmer shacks in the Third Ward built in the 1930s. With money from the National Endowment for the Arts and the Elizabeth Firestone Graham Foundation, and using volunteers from a number of organizations, Lowe mobilized people across the city to restore the neighborhood.

According to the article, these homes today form the core of Project Row Houses, one of the most original and ambitious works of art of the past century. Eight of the shacks are designated studio and exhibition spaces, while seven others are devoted to the Young Mothers Residential Program, which hosts single women trying to finish school. No one group of inhabitants is separate from the other. The young mothers and the artists are integrally involved in each others' lives and creativity.

Inspired by the Project Row Houses, Theaster Gates invested money from the sales of his artwork to buy up and transform properties in his Chicago community. In 2009, he acquired the empty house next door to his home, turning it into a library and stocking it with the 14,000 vol-umes he bought from the nearby Prairie Avenue Bookshop, which was closing. When the neighboring Dr. Wax record store closed, he bought the inventory and turned it into a collection in the former candy store, which he renamed the Listening House. He also created a screening room for black cinema.

In 2012 Gates struck a deal with the city and bought a neo-Classical ruin that had once been a bank for $1. To raise money for its restoration, he took marble slabs that had once been part of the building and imprinted them with the motto "IN ART WE TRUST." Then he sold them for $50,000 each as "bonds" to fund the renovation of the building. The building is now open and is home to the company collection of the late John H. Johnson, publisher of the African-American magazines *Ebony* and *Jet.*

Mark Bradford's imprint is in Leimert Park where he grew up, only seven miles from downtown Los Angeles. Recipient of a MacArthur Genius Grant in 2009, Bradford's challenge was to bring creativity to the community, so people didn't need to travel to experience the arts. He cofounded the Art + Practice Foundation with art collector and philanthropist Eileen Harris Norton and neighborhood activist Allan DiCastro. It's located in several buildings and has a 4,000-square-foot exhibition space at the center of the campus. Along with a focus on the arts, the center, through an affiliation with the RightWay Foundation, offers job training and mental health services to the neighborhood's foster youth.

These three artists have created great change and possibility in their communities. They have inspired each other and their projects continue to inspire and assist great numbers of people. And it all started with one high school student asking "Why don't you help fix the problem instead of painting it?"

Today I received an email about a company that was just started to help children understand the importance of empathy and being kind. The founder, Lily Yeh, a mother of two, was looking for volunteer opportunities her children could participate in, and when she found none, she started Little Loving Hands.[19] Every month, they send a package to subscribers that contains a kit with information about an organization in need of support and a craft project for the kids to do while learning who, why and how they are helping. Each child also receives a collectible button and certificate of achievement. Included in the kit is a prepaid return envelope to send the child's finished craft as a donation to those in need.

Projects have included stuffed toys that are being included in the welcome bags given to patients staying at the Ronald McDonald House Charities as well as accessories for children with fallen, deployed, and injured parents that have served in the military.

In every community, individuals are stepping up like Lily Yeh, like these featured artists, and *doing* something to add value to our society. They live with the awareness that we all need each other, that we have unique gifts to share and that our lives work best when are we actively and generously engaged with others.

In order to reach our spiritual maturity, as individuals and as a human family, we must reconnect the heart and brain, becoming as fluent in feelings as we are in facts. Our lives stem from our beliefs, and if our beliefs are not rooted in affection, if they lack the heft of emotion, the power of passion, they are nothing but a barren field of brainwaves.

WHOSE LIFE ARE YOU LIVING?

Where you are right now—in that relationship, in that job, in that house—might all be tied to someone else's creation. Perhaps you weren't paying attention to your own words and thoughts and got swept up in someone else's desire. If you're not causing your own life to unfold in a certain way, who is? When we manage to focus consciously on what we desire, speak openly of the things we are creating, give our time to the activities that make us happy, then we are being true to our creative calling.

And it is not just our personal lives that we are creating. We are attendants at the wake of the old way, and each of us—through our actions, our thoughts, our work and relationships—is midwifing a new world into existence. *This* is our destiny, our meaning, our purpose, and when we come to our days with this awareness, when we wake up to this tremendous privilege, when we sense the oak in the acorn of our beings, then we will have the energy to move mountains and shift the tides.

It is an illusion that we are powerless. It is an illusion that someone else is responsible. It is an illusion that we cannot transcend these dualities and differences that are making a mockery of democracy. We are the people. This is our world. Every movement that ever led to any change in this ever-evolving civilization grew like a seed from one person's imagination. And what did that person have? A deeply-rooted sense of what's right; a commitment to heart-sharing, to bridge-building; an ability to inspire, *to breathe life into* the hearts and minds of others.

Transformation originates in people who see a better way or a fairer world, people who reveal themselves, disclose their dreams, and unfold their hopes in the presence of others. And this very unfolding, this revelation of raw, unharnessed desire, this deep longing to be a force for good in the world is what inspires others to feel their own longings, to remember their own purpose, and to act, perhaps for the first time, in accordance with their inner spirit.

The greatest courage that is called for is the courage to be real. When we are real, the rusty padlocks to our hearts break open and people can enter in. When we are real, the ice floes melt, the dams break, and all the feelings we are meant to feel run like rivers through our system, bringing life, bringing hope. The solutions to our crises are already here. They exist in our relationships, in our stories, in our tender intimacies, and it is through the expression of these things that we will one day live into the answers we seek at this time. To be creators, we need not know the answers. The currency of creativity is wonder. It is not-knowing and always finding.

Our power comes from our ability to create our experience, harvest its lessons, reap its wisdom. It is a work of alchemy to turn the lead of grief into the gold of gratitude. It is at once a gift of grace and a show of faith. Each of us knows what no one else knows because no one else has lived our lives, seen what we've seen, felt what we've felt. The poet Rumi writes, "The throbbing vein will take you further than any thinking." This is a great clue.

It's always the story of an emotional experience that captivates others. Disembodied thoughts that are not rooted in story are platitudes, empty calories. Every good teacher, preacher, lecturer knows that it's story that fires the imagination, feeds the brain, nourishes the heart. When Rumi said "Stop learning, start knowing," we take it to mean that we are already sitting on a gold mine. We have a stockpile of experience to work with. We need only become silent enough, mindful enough, to focus our thoughts and create our masterpieces. If we simply stopped, sat still, revisited the stories of our life, teased out the conflicts and what they taught us, we would see the wealth of experience that dwells in our flesh and bones.

Right this moment each one of us is in the process of evolving ourselves forward. Our success in creating extraordinary lives are proportionate to the conviction we bring to the table. If we have trained ourselves to be mindful, we have a great advantage. If we are committed to a practice of daily silence—even if it's a short period of time—we are set up for success because our receptive, intuitive channels are open to Intelligence-at-Large. We are finite beings communing with Infinity. Awareness of this miracle fuels us, magnifies our potential, expands our possibilities.

We cannot improve our consciousness with supplements or medicine. We cannot hire the job out. We cannot buy it. It is the one thing we grow through practice, discipline, commitment, by paying attention and taking our words seriously. There is a great potential living in every thought and whether it is released or not is up to us.

Henri Bergson writes in *Creative Evolution,*

Organic evolution resembles the evolution of a consciousness, in which the past presses against the present and causes the upspringing of a new form of consciousness, incommensurable with its antecedents...The philosophy of the future will only be built up by the collective and progressive effort of many thinkers, of many observers also, completing, correcting, and improving one another.[20]

This upspringing is occurring now, this new form of consciousness is being born into the world every day, not only with the birth of each new infant, but with the rebirth of each of us as we resurrect into the creators, prophets, teachers and healers we are born to be.

CHAPTER 9

———— ⌒⟶ ————

CONNECT THE DOTS: WHY YOUR CREATIVITY AND SPIRITUALITY GO ARM IN ARM

Freeing our thinking from the limitations of its biological form is essentially a spiritual undertaking.

RAY KURZWEIL

THE SYMBIOSIS OF SPIRITUALITY AND CREATIVITY

ONE DAY IN the fierce cold of upstate New York, on an early morning in March, I took my camera and left for a walk through the woods of our hundred acre property. I had survived the —20 degree days of winter, the relentless splitting and hauling of wood for the fire, the long hours inside when it was too cold to walk. But on this day, I couldn't see my breath when I woke up in the morning. It was warming up, so I headed out.

There was still snow on the ground and the crunch of my boots echoed through the woods. I was thrilled already, just to be walking, when I spotted an array of trillium that sent joy through my veins. I crawled down on my belly, took off my gloves, set my aperture to f16. I put the camera on my 6 inch tripod, slowed down the shutter speed, and focused in on the trinity of leaves. Lying there in the snow, I crawled from plant to plant, looking for the best light, the brightest leaves. When I stood up again, an hour had passed. In all that time, I felt not a moment of cold or discomfort. Crawling around in the snow, no aches, no pains. Just the happiness of being, of feeling one with nature, suspended in time.

This is similar to the experience that Ruth and I have on our yearly photo sabbaticals. Whether we're in a rainforest, a desert, the mountains or the ocean's shore, we are excited and alert. Our attention doesn't waver, our focus doesn't soften, our awe never fades because this planet provides a constant array of ever-changing beauty. We are in love with the moment, and it is there, in that infinitely unfolding present, that each of us feels our own sense of wonder, our connection to the divine. We are bound to Earth and the force that created it.

Driving down the back roads, I'll hear Ruth shouting out to get my attention.

"Oh my God, look at that garden. It's so Monet!"

Or passing through a country landscape, she might compare it to a Cezanne or Seurat. A golden light will fall on something in just the right way, and I hear:

"That is so totally impressionistic. Look at that. Isn't it amazing?"

She will pull off into a field, stop the car, grab her tripod and spend a half-hour photographing the decaying remnants of a caved-in barn. She burrows in with her macro lens, lost in a world of texture, shadow and light. I view the scene through a wide-angle lens, seeing pasture, mountain, well.

For both of us, the earth is our temple. The moment is sacred. There is something spiritual about our creativity, and something creative about our spirituality. Both of us grew up in religions that did not foster self-expression or original thinking. Both of us are true to a daily spiritual practice of solitude and silence. We each enjoy an unmediated experience of the sacred. We each give a tremendous amount of time to projects that serve the human family, both globally and in our local and national communities. Both of us were raised in families that always had enough, but never had anything extra.

"My family was affected by the war, depression, alcoholism," said Ruth. "I was an only child and was left to raise myself. No one ever asked about my report card, whether I did my homework or not. We had no books or magazines in the house. My parents were not educated and never involved themselves in my life. I was on my own and made plenty of big mistakes growing up, but one thing happened that got me on the right path."

"I was working full-time as a showroom manager for a carpet company in Los Angeles and taking care of my mother who had heart disease. The president of the company saw some promise in me and offered to pay for my education. When it was time to pay him back, he wouldn't accept a dime. The only thing he asked was that I do the same for others when I could. And from then on, I've been doing just that. It started with volunteering and fundraising for non-profits, but now with the Westreich Foundation, I am able to have a lot greater impact."

Ruth believes that the body, mind and spirit are inseparable, and that spiritually we are linked to every other living thing. Those beliefs inform both her artistic creativity and her creative approach to changing paradigms in the way health is created and treated in our culture. "I didn't have a master plan. In the beginning I felt like a careening piece on a carom board, but I kept doing the next indicated thing. I've always worked for the greater good and now I can see it paying off. I trusted my internal guidance system and it didn't let me down."

Earle Coleman, in his book *Creativity and Spirituality*, writes that art and spirituality "find their deep family resemblance in the yearning for harmony" and that the common denominator between the two is the "quest for oneness." Coleman addresses the similarities between the mystical experience and the creative experience, asserting that "art and religion are complementary responses to the quest for self-realization."[1]

Spirituality and creativity are like fraternal twins. They are not identical in expression, but they come from the same source. The spirituality we speak of is the invisible force that is greater than anything that exists and *behind* all existence itself. It's what Einstein spoke of when he said, "Something deeply hidden had to be behind things." Or what poet David Whyte might have had in mind when he said, "The conversation is not *about* the relationship. The conversation *is* the relationship."

Our creativity *is* our spirituality. It is an expression of what we care about, what we believe in. What we create—our lives, our days, our stories—these are products of our thoughts and convictions. I will not create dissonance if I begin my day with prayers for peace. I will not create war if I am a committed pacifist. I will not make obscene images if I see all things as holy.

The spirituality we speak of *is* the Creative Force—it is the cosmos expanding through us, Supreme Intelligence broadcasting Itself through the channels of our bodies and minds. We are agents of evolution, carriers of consciousness, and our creations convey the majestic beauty, the sacred elegance, the profound complexities of our human experience. Creativity is our spirituality in running shoes.

While religions are about beliefs that tend to separate us from each other, spirituality is about our oneness as children of the universe. Spirituality is the meal, one might say, while religion is the menu. Spirituality is the music washing over our cells, religion is the score propped up on the music stand. For some, the two are like sea and the salt, intertwined in an organic marriage. For others—those who describe themselves as "spiritual but not religious"—most of the religious beliefs they inherited as children have been abandoned, and they are creating a faith day by day based on what they are learning from their lived experience.

A Jesuit priest once said in my first theology class, "Your religion is the set of beliefs passed down to you from the church. Your spirituality is something *you* create based on your commitments and ultimate concerns. You have to know what you are committed to in order to have a living faith." At the age of eighteen, sitting in a classroom with 29 other novices training to be nuns, this challenge unnerved me. We had always been taught *what* to think, but never *how* to think. How was I to know what I was committed to? It took Father Grabys the whole semester to mentor us in spiritual consciousness as we put our beliefs on the back burner and set about to discover who we were and what concerns guided us.

In 1969, I identified the following as my ultimate commitments: to be a maker of peace, a bearer of light, and a voice for justice. All these years later, that has never wavered. And all of my creations spring from that well, rise up from those roots. Whether it's music, photographs, stories, or relationships, whatever I create is connected to who I am spiritually. I may be more discernibly an activist than Ruth—who refers to herself as an "accidental activist"—but underneath everything, we both feel connected to a power greater than our own and committed to the good of the whole.

THE RENEWAL INHERENT IN SPIRITUALITY

Ruth said to me the other day, "When I take my walk in the morning, I have two really different experiences. When I look down or straight ahead, I feel really connected to the earth. I feel like a part of everything, like nature itself in another form. Then, when I look up, I feel like a tiny particle in a vast cosmos. Still connected, but not in the same way I am connected to the earth. I think it's the combination of both those feelings that make it feel spiritual; it's the two things coming together— heaven and earth becoming one."

Ruth was raised by fundamentalist Methodists—no makeup, no dancing, no drinking or gambling. When she married, she converted to Judaism. Neither of those religions inspired her, informed her as much as her morning walks through nature. Ruth's spiritual practice has become those daily jaunts through the woods and walkways. She claims it as her time to be connected, to get "grounded," to be in communion with the invisible forces and fields all around her. Without this commitment, she would not be the creator she is, for there is an intimate connection between the two.

Over 2000 years ago, the Roman poet Horace said, "The purpose of art is to inform and delight." Over the years, art has played a key role in providing images of spiritual experience. Every existing medium has been called out in the service of religion. Stories of faith have been handed down through stained glass, bronze, music, literature, plays, mosaics, murals. Egyptian tombs have been filled with artwork depicting gods and goddesses and the opulent afterlife. The walls of temples, mosques and cathedrals around the world reverberate with the energetic imprint of what has been emotionally evoked there over the centuries. Art is the medium that best connects the common to the Transcendent, the mortal to the Immortal.

Think of the books on your bookshelves and how they tie you to ages past and ages to come. Think of the poems that have put you in another's shoes, turned another's sorrow into tears in your eyes. Think of how the songs from your youth make you want to shake your hips or do the twist. Think of how many times you've sat in a dark theater and cried your eyes out in the company of three hundred others doing the same. Creation is worthy of our tears. It is an unfolding of the new. Something ushering forth from nothing.

Physicist Michio Kaku once said, as a way of describing the beginning of the universe, "When Nothing became unstable, particles of Something started to form." It is often the case with humans. We become unstable, at times, and from that unknowing, from that dark cavern of curiosity emerges a new answer in a new form—unannounced, uninvited, a new creation. It is a miracle, birthed from our originality and imagination. It is life giving birth to life, the universe expanding extravagantly, exponentially, through us— through our thoughts, through our hands, through our sweat and service.

It is nearly impossible to separate creativity from spirituality, except to say perhaps that conscious or not, one creates; whereas one's spirituality is rooted in the ground of consciousness. We are creative by default, but we are not spiritual by default. We create our lives, our relationships, our circumstances with our thoughts and our words. It happens every day whether we are enlightened or not.

Being spiritual, in our opinion, involves commitment, conviction, action. One determines what one is ultimately committed to and then acts in accordance with that commitment. It does not happen in the absence of thought or consciousness. It is value-laden, on purpose, unique to us. In many cases they are intertwined, like the vocal cords and voice. One might imagine spirituality is the breath, creativity is the word. But this will resonate only to those for whom this is true. Others will have different feelings, and those feelings will be accurate as well.

The creative milieu is a place where all of us should feel safe to express what's deep within, whether it's light or dark. We are all evolving, but none of us at the same rate. We're like an oak tree in October. Its leaves change at different rates, at different times. One tree will have an array of green, gold, orange, yellow and red leaves on it. None is better than the other. They are evolving and changing in their own time. Our experiences have been unique and our knowings will be unique, as all true wisdom is gained from experience. What we have in common is that we are all moving forward.

In his book, *Concerning the Spiritual in Art,* artist Wassily Kandinsky wrote:

> Literature, music and art are the most sensitive spheres in which this spiritual revolution makes itself felt. They reflect the dark picture of the present time and show the importance of what was at first only a little point of light noticed by the few. Perhaps they even grow dark in their turn, but they turn away from the soulless life of the present toward those substances and ideas that give free scope to the non-material strivings of the soul.[2]

Many artists see their art in spiritual terms. Many attempt to create work which expresses a concern for things beyond the material, which incorporates a hope for impact that is positive and enduring. When artists allow themselves to be prophetic, when revelation takes shape through them, they actually can have a powerful influence on the consciousness of a community.

Alex Grey is an artist whose images of the transcendent are revelatory and mystical. I was changed forever the day I walked into his Sacred Mirrors exhibition in La Jolla, California. He brought to the canvas images that represented my deepest hopes and most fervent faith. He painted in the lines that connect us. He literally illustrated the etheric web that weaves us together. His work was huge, both in scope and impact.

In his book, *The Mission of Art,* he writes:

> The artist's soul is a psychic antenna tuned to the needs of the world soul. Mostly, artists remain unconscious of the nature of creative forces operating through them, except to feel the tormenting drive and joyful satisfaction of their work. Creation is the Mystery itself. Wise artists respond to the call of creation by peering into their own hearts....By touching our deepest center, great art transmits the condition of the soul and awakens the healing power of spirit. Art is communion of one soul to another, offered through the symbolic language of form and content.[3]

Though we have focused on the artistic aspect of creativity in this chapter, let us remember that the primary creation we are each shaping is our very life. The steps are similar. As the creator of your life, you peer into your own heart, tune into its deep desire, tend to your thoughts and align them with your vision, imagine new ways of sharing your soul/self with others.

My Aunt Joyce, a recent widow, knits constantly because it soothes her. Whenever I visit her, she is in her chair knitting. When I ask what she is working on, I know her answer will bring me joy. "Oh, I'm making baby booties for Mercy Hospital...I'm making caps for the newborn preemies at House of the Good Samaritan...I'm making sweaters and afghans for the church for families who need them." She knits when dinner is cooking, when the Yankees are playing, when her kids are there making Manhattans. I wouldn't be surprised if she knits her prayers right into those mittens and socks, doing what she can to bring joy and safety to the little ones who'll be wearing them.

Our creative work demands our whole attention, and is healing and holy *because* of that. When I am writing music, I cannot feel sorrow. When

I am photographing, telling stories, writing sonnets, I cannot be sad. I can only feel the energy of creation surging through me. I can only be attentive, captivated, enlivened.

When Ruth makes jewelry or works on a painting, she is lifted up from the world's crises and dropped into the promised land of here and now. All her attention goes into design, color, shapes, the practicalities of making a thing work in every way. And it is that focus, that steadfast footing in the present moment that brings creativity's saving grace to all creators. To add the beauty and blessing of nature to the equation adds exponentially to the joy. Ruth writes:

> I'm not religious in any way, but working on something creative always has spiritual benefits for me. I don't necessarily think of it as "spiritual," but on some deep level, I think all the right components are there. When I create, I'm usually in solitude. I'm in a reflective space, consciously open to ideas from the universe. I usually have beautiful music playing in the background. I feel in communion, somehow—like I'm not alone. I am not praying for anything, but rather I feel generally joyful for the idea exchange, joyful to be there without all the usual worries and timelines. In my studio, it feels like what I wish church felt like for people. Creativity is holy to me because it makes me feel whole and healed.

In our survey, when we asked about the connection between creativity and spirituality, a vast majority of respondents answered in the positive. Nearly everyone feels a relationship between the two, though it is difficult to say why. Perhaps it's because both activities involve the soul, the journey inward, the encounter with the Great Unknown. One decides to create, then dives into the darkness, surrendering the will and opening to the way that is only shown to us after we've begun.

There is a great deal of trust involved—trust in the voice beneath our own, trust in our ability to get out of the way, trust in the stories that

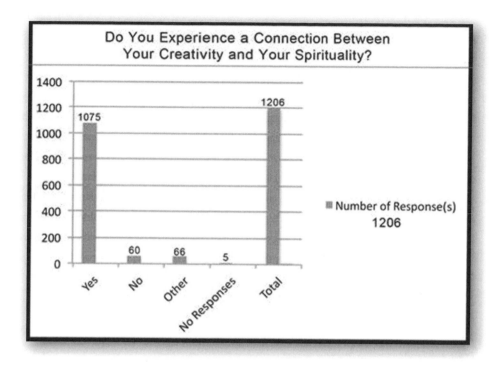

knock at our doors. Creativity is work of the heart, unrelated to the economy of our ordinary lives. It is not about money, or success, or ego. It is a calling from the spirit, a chance at one of life's powerful experiences: to make something whole from the pieces of our lives. It is our way of harvesting our adventures, mining our joys and sorrows for the jewels they contain. May Sarton once wrote, "I suppose I have written novels to find out what I thought about something, and poems to find out what I felt about something." E. M. Forster said similarly, "How can I know what I think till I see what I say?"

Every morning I begin my day with a period of silence. I reflect on whatever comes to mind as I gaze at my candle. I enter into the non-dual world of complete and utter possibility. I do not allow thoughts of right or wrong, yes or no. I marry each thought to its opposite as quickly as I can. I am training my brain for the oneness that my soul already knows. At the end of my reflection time, I write a poem in my journal that tries to crystallize the experience, that speaks of the journey in a metaphoric way. It is similar to Meister Eckhart's idea: "To be properly expressed, a thing must proceed from within, moved by its form."

There would be no poem without the silence, for it takes its shape, finds its form, in those moments of reflection. The poem is conceived in the union of past and present, as I merge what I learned to believe with what I know from my life. I am not railing against the wrongs. I am creating something new that refers back to the old and evolves it forward. I am not worried about judgment or criticism. That will come inevitably if my work is beautiful enough, sturdy enough, enduring enough to make its way into the hearts of people. There will be feelings and responses and discomfort and joy and I will hear about it—and all that says to me is that a powerful thing occurred. I created something that *moved* people. And that is what I set out to do.

ART'S RAPTURE

When we let the spirit or voice of our creations interweave with our own thoughts of what it is and where it is headed, we engage in the deep mystery of art. This is its rapture. It is flesh in a dance with spirit, the ultimate embrace out of which comes a work as pure as our intent, as fresh and wild as our imagination. There is more power here than anywhere else.

Igor Stravisnky wrote in his *Memoirs and Commentaries,* "My knowledge is activity. I discover it as I work, and know it while I am discovering it, but only in a very different way before and after. I do not try to *think* in advance. I only start to work and hope to leap a little in my spirit." This is the challenge to us: *to make of our knowledge an activity.* To transform the events of our lives into stories that show the pattern behind all our crazy choices, all our wayward actions and wrong turns. Because the truth is, we needed those turns to get where we are today. As Hafiz said, "This place where you are right now God circled on a map for you."

The relationship between creativity and spirituality is like yin and yang, light and dark. One is an inward journey into the deep caves of mystery. The other is a journey outward, from the core to the cosmos. One is silent, the other expressive. One demands movement from our eyes, our hands, our legs. One demands stillness, sitting, receiving not transmitting.

There is no definitive way to excel in either milieu. There is no reason to be competitive, to judge or to blame—either ourselves or others.

In the matter of creativity and spirituality, the best we can do is acknowledge their intimacy, foster their closeness, learn their language and translate their messages. In the practice of both, we engage with a power greater than ourselves, open to a wisdom deeper than any we have ever known. Mysteries are afoot when we sit in silence or begin to create. Earth wobbles in its orbit when we dare to speak the beauty we know. This is the power of our spirit in action, our soul enfleshed. This is our moment to heal what's broken, to bring light to the dark.

CHAPTER 10

—————— ✦ ——————

STAND UP, STAND OUT: WHY CONSCIOUS CREATIVITY IS THE NEW ACTIVISM

Compassion is an unstable emotion.
It needs to be translated into action, or it withers.
SUSAN SONTAG

WHEN I FIRST met Ruth, fifteen years ago, the conversation went something like this:

"Hi, I'm Jan Phillips. I'm a writer, an artist, and an activist."

"I'm Ruth Westreich. I'm an artist, but I don't identify as an activist."

"Oh, O.K., I said, thinking it odd that a woman with a reputation for being one of San Diego's premier social philanthropists didn't think of herself as an activist. She was probably spending more hours a week on social projects than I was, but the label wasn't a fit for her.

I'd been an activist since1972 when I had my first experience with homophobia and decided to speak out about gay issues. Activism back then was synonymous with protest, with demonstrations and rallies against war, nuclear proliferation, racial segregation, inequality for women, anti-gay legislation. In the 1960s and 70s, American families across the nation watched the Viet Nam war unfold in our living rooms. Images of death and violence broke into our homes and hearts every night on the evening news.

When the Civil Rights Movement was in full swing, photos from the South migrated north, unfolding *what* was happening as well as *why*. Images from Saigon to Selma drove a generation of activists out of our homes and into the streets. I was one of those activists. Ruth was a homemaker raising two children to be socially-conscious and compassionate people. Two expressions of a common hope.

As a young photographer, I documented every rally I attended and created a slideshow called *Focus on Peace*. It was an emotional, upbeat chronicle of the anti-nuclear, anti-war protests across the U.S. and Canada. It featured children to octogenarians and people from diverse faith traditions, ethnic backgrounds and cultures. The soundtrack was an international children's choir singing *Let There Be Peace on Earth*. I presented this slideshow wherever I could, and in the early eighties I saved $5000 for a year-long peace pilgrimage around the world. I traveled as an artist/activist through thirteen countries, sharing my photos and creating occasions for people to come together and talk about what it means to make peace where we live.

I presented at at the Nagasaki Association for the Promotion of Peace to a group of forty *hibakusha*, survivors of the atomic bomb dropped on August 9, 1945. The survivors had gathered to see a film made by a Japanese director who had acquired some recently declassified footage from the U.S. military. After the film, I was going to share my slides and do a brief talk. The deputy director of the museum, Mr. Terumasa Matsunaga, sat beside me and the lights went out for the film. It started out in color, panning the beautiful gardens and statues in the Nagasaki Peace Park. Then it cut to black and white and we were looking out of the cockpit of the *Enola Gay*, the B-29 bomber that dropped the bomb on Nagasaki.

Everyone in the audience gasped. It was horrifying to see the bomb falling, the detonation, the massive mushroom shaped cloud billowing into the sky. The film went on to include footage taken from the ground in Nagasaki, shortly after the detonation. The area had been obliterated and people were wandering around calling out for family members amidst the wreckage. Some of the survivors saw themselves on the screen. Some cried out. Some started to weep. Mr. Matsunaga, the museum president sitting next to me, put his head down on the table and started to sob. The sounds of their sorrow filled the room as we witnessed the rerun of a nuclear holocaust.

When it was over, no one moved. No one turned on the lights. We sat together in silence till the weeping stopped. Then, when the lights came up, Mr. Matsunaga took me to the front of the room. When I stood before the survivors, I started to cry. I said how sorry I was. I said I was dedicating my life to the end of war. I spoke of the millions who were doing the same. I didn't have any answers, I said, but I had some pictures that I hoped would help.

The slideshow went on, and the hibakusha watched intently, seeing a multitude of banners and signs written in both Japanese and English: *Never Another Nuclear War; No More Nagasaki; Hiroshima, Nagasaki, Never Again!* They saw contingents of Japanese activists, scores of Buddhist monks, cities and parks filled with people who shared a vision—images they never imagined in their wildest fantasies. They became aware for the first time that people on the other side of the world knew what happened and committed to it not happening again. At the end of the show, many of the survivors cried again, only this time for joy.

I had a small tape recorder with me and asked if any of them would like to come up and say something in the microphone. Everyone in the room stood up. They formed a line, and each one said nearly the same thing into the recorder: "Thank you for letting us know we are not alone." Tsuyo Kataoka, a survivor I interviewed later, said, "All these years we thought no one cared. We thought what happened to us did not matter to anyone. After the bomb, I lost my sight, my hearing, everyone in my family. My eyesight returned, my hearing returned, but not my hope, until today. Your photographs brought hope back to my heart. All those people became my new family."

What happened to those survivors in 1945 caused an eruption in consciousness around the world, the emergence of a community dedicated to preventing another holocaust. I was a part of that community. I was against war, against violence, against nuclear weapons, and I publicly proclaimed that. That was how my activism looked thirty years ago. Today it looks entirely different.

One person is never going to single-handedly bring an end to war, but this one person shared photos that changed the lives of those survivors.

This one person brought stories of what had changed since that dreadful day, stories of a movement that got its start on August 9, 1945, when a few individuals stood up and said "This will not happen again on my watch." For the first time in nearly 40 years, those survivors realized how much their lives mattered to people around the world, and they couldn't stop thanking me for sharing this news. I did not embark on that peace pilgrimage as a teacher, an educator. I did not talk about the number of Cruise or Pershing missiles we had. I was out there as a storyteller, and the stories my pictures told were worth thousands of words.

When the Berlin Wall came down a few years after my journey, I spent a day remembering that time—all the countries I'd visited, the thousands of people I'd interacted with, the hopes that were seeded in so many hearts—and I thought: that wall didn't come down because of one or two superheroes. It came down because so many of us took a stand, acted on our beliefs, and felt so strongly a new day coming that it couldn't help but arrive.

The activism of the sixties, seventies and eighties was primarily an activism of dissent. More than anything, it was a registration of public protest. We addressed the shadow side of our own society and spoke out against it. Today, activism is taking a turn toward the light. The question is not just what are we *against,* but what are we *for?*

How can we create more meaningful lives for ourselves, act on what we believe in, work with others to create sustainable communities? How do we become more active agents, more mindful creators in general? How to we remember that life isn't happening *to* us, but *through* us? That our thoughts, our words, and our feelings are the seeds that sprout each day into the beautiful things we call our lives. A peaceful world is created by individuals who make a habit of creating peaceful lives. That calls for practice, discipline, commitment. That is an act of consciousness. That is the activism of today. We are activating our awareness, our compassion. We are actively and mindfully creating our relationships and families.

Movements of the past have had their charismatic leaders— Susan B. Anthony, Rachel Carson, Dr. Martin Luther King, Jr., Malcolm X, Cesar

Chavez, Harvey Milk, Gloria Steinem—but the movements of today are more dispersed and independent. Paul Hawken, in his book *Blessed Unrest,* calls this phenomenon the largest social movement in history without a name.[1] He refers to a massive mobilization of 1-2 million groups and organizations working toward ecological sustainability and social justice. There are no manifestos or doctrines, but simply the uprising of a global humanitarian movement from the bottom up. There are millions of people who don't even think of themselves as activists who are creating solutions to social problems in every imaginable milieu.

It is as if people are finally understanding the Lakota prayer: *Mitakuye Oyasin,* meaning *All My Relations* or *We Are All Related.* It is as if more and more are tuned into the idea that any action that is not good for everyone, for the creatures, or for the earth is not a wise action. Awareness of our interconnectedness is moving from our subconscious to our social consciousness.

This statement turns our prevailing paradigm on its head. It's a pithy reminder that we are intricately connected as global citizens, like it or not. Joseph Campbell, in *Myths to Live By,* offers an image for a new paradigm. He writes:

> We are the children of this beautiful planet. We were not delivered into it by some god, but have come forth from it. We are its eyes and mind, its seeing and its thinking. And the earth, together with its sun, came forth, we are told, from a nebula; and that nebula, in turn, from space. No wonder then, if its laws and our laws are the same. Likewise our depths are the depths of space...We can no longer hold our loves at home and project our aggressions elsewhere; for on this spaceship Earth there is no 'elsewhere' any more. And no mythology that continues to speak or to teach of 'elsewheres' and 'outsiders' meets the requirement of this hour."[2]

As if in some sort of cosmic mid-course correction, the issue of "elsewheres" and "outsiders" is pressing upon the human consciousness like never before in history. People desperate for food, shelter, work are showing up en masse at borders around the world and nations wrestle with a crisis of conscience as thousands of starving migrants knock at their door. The whole world is watching on the daily news as the evolution of humanity unfolds before us with all its terrors and triumphs. Activists are speaking out on all sides, helping to shape a conversation that considers all dimensions. Each of us contributes to the final outcome in an immeasurable manner, both by what we say and what we fail to say.

Our public imagination, our social conscience, is undergoing a transformation from local to global. We are coming to understand that our thoughts, feelings, and words transform themselves into the very culture we are part of, the very future we inherit. They matter deeply. They have consequences. They are the tools of our creativity, the colors that become the painting.

A circle of compassion widened in San Diego, California after the murder of a 20 year old Muslim man, Tarik Khamisa, by a 14 year old gang member. International financial consultant Azim Khamisa said that the news of his son's death was like the detonation of a nuclear bomb inside his heart. "What is different about this story is that while I obviously had compassion for my son, somehow in my heart I felt compassion for the fourteen year old who took my son's life. There were victims at both ends of the gun—Tarik, a victim of Tony, and Tony, a victim of society," said Khamisa in an interview at his home.[3]

Nine months after losing his son, Khamisa started a foundation in his son's honor, and at the first meeting the assistant District Attorney who had handled his son's case was present. Khamisa asked the ADA to be introduced to Ples Felix, Tony's guardian and grandfather, and they eventually met in the Public Defender's office. "I told him I didn't feel any animosity toward him or his grandson, that I was concerned about him and all the other kids who are growing up in this violent world, and that I started this foundation to help provide some solutions. I invited him to the second meeting and we've been working together since 1995," said Khamisa.

"The first feeling I had was really jubilant rejoicing because it was the answer to my prayers," said Felix, a former Green Beret who did two tours of duty in Viet Nam. "When I first found out that my grandson was responsible for murdering an innocent soul, I began immediately to pray for the Khamisa family, and for the opportunity to meet them so I could express my sympathy and commit myself to them, to help in any way I could with the loss. When the time came, I felt nervous and uncertain, but when I looked into Azim's eyes, I didn't see hatred, or any of the things you'd expect to see from a man who lost his son at the hands of my grandson. He shook my hand, told me his plans for the foundation, and asked if I would join him."

Since then, the Tarik Khamisa Foundation has worked with over 500,000 gang age youth teaching them conflict resolution and alternatives to violence. Tony and Azim have met face to face and Azim has offered him a job at the foundation when Tony gets out of prison. Both Ples and Azim write to Tony frequently, and so do hundreds of school-children write to say that seeing him take responsibility for what he did has helped them to rethink violence, to stay away from gangs, to make better choices.

"By saving Tony, which in my heart of hearts I know we will, think about how many kids Tony will save," said Khamisa. And it is not just children, but adults who have been similarly transformed by the actions of these two men. When they went to receive the prestigious Common Ground Award in Washington, D.C., Azim was approached by a woman whose son was also murdered. "How do you forgive them?" she asked, admitting that she was struggling to find compassion in her heart.

Azim responded by saying there were three major parts to forgiveness: first, acknowledge that you've been wronged; second, give up all the resulting resentment; and finally, reach out to the perpetrator with love and compassion. "Then the woman met Ples and you could see the electricity," he said. "Later the woman wrote me, saying it was because of Ples and you that I have reached out to the family of my son's perpetrator. Thank you for the healing."

This is transformation. This is activism at its most creative. This is original thinking—saying no to conditioned responses that keep us in the trap of duality, and saying yes to what appears to be "other." The Tariq Khamisa Foundation (TKF) was seeded by a tragedy, but when Azim and Ples reached out to each other, a powerful new entity was created and it has changed the face of San Diego. The foundation sponsors over 25 community service activities for youth. They partner with schools and recreation centers to host ten week summer projects for teens. They organize interactive presentations known as Violence Impact Assemblies that use video, discussions and real stories to encourage reflection on emotions and actions regarding violence. Through their Mentorship Program, over 500 youth are mentored each year, with each teen receiving an average of eight hours of attention monthly.

Not only does TKF offer a multitude of opportunities for teens to be involved in the community, it offers an opportunity for adults to volunteer as mentors, bringing value and purpose to their own lives in the process. Every American community has non-profits and organizations serving populations with specific needs. And every citizen who contributes time and energy to the success of these programs is an activist who is acting for the public good. There are no signs to carry. No enemies to blame. Just the diligent work of finding ourselves in the "other," and doing what we can to share the load.

In some circles, this is known as "enlightened self interest." It means when we serve others, we serve ourselves. As it says in the *Course in Miracles,* "Giving is receiving." In this era of technological triumph, our interdependence and connectedness is more obvious than ever. Physicist Menas Kafatos writes: "Nature has shown us that our concept of reality, consisting of units that can be considered as separate from each other, is fundamentally wrong." Since we are composed of cells, molecules, atoms and sub-atomic particles, this makes *each of us* part of one indivisible whole, interconnected. and interdependent. Acting for the benefit of another would simultaneously be self-serving, as would harming another also bring harm to ourselves.

If this is true, why do our levels of violence against each other continue to escalate? What will it take to raise awareness of our interdependence? Biologist E.O. Wilson writes in *The Social Conquest of Earth*, "We have created a Star Wars civilization with stone age emotions, medieval institutions and god-like technology." We are like toddlers emotionally, PhDs technologically, and non-thinking termites collectively. The old myth of a Sky God who makes everything happen is giving way to an understanding that it is WE who have the whole world in our hands, and yet people frivolously abdicate their creative power.

Those who are *not* abdicating—who are consciously involved in the creation of their lives and this culture—are the activists among us. They are *acting* for the benefit of the whole. They are creating conversations of consequence, instigating group discussions, evolving their own and others' social and spiritual intelligence. They create community, change, culture.

They may not think of themselves as activists. They may simply have a point of view, an idea they want to share. They want it to be as beautiful as possible so people will be attracted to it and enter into it. They imagine someone engaging with it. They imagine it making a difference. They hope, perhaps, to cause some shift in the viewer, to cause movement. They create something that has not existed before, that has an energy of its own, that could alter the reality of the one who finds it, and they put it out into the world. This is activism of a new order. It is action taken with the intention to cause change, add light, birth something new. It is more an invitation than a protest.

In a phone interview with Anne Laker, founding member of the Big Car Collaborative in Indianapolis, I learned something new about activism in the 21st century. She was sharing about some of the creative activities the group offered for people to get involved with at the Spark Monument Circle. "We noticed it was hard to approach and engage with people at the circle because so many were wearing ear buds. So we designed an experience that was comfortable, free, and surprising," said Laker. "We offered chess and ping pong, music by local artists, conversational bistro-style seating on platforms known as parklets, and the Wagon of Wonders, a mobile, interactive art unit and pop-up public space. We also had a listening booth where a person could go to get ten minutes of pure attention from one of our artists."

She also shared that they meet frequently with city planners, and work with CEOs for Cities, a national group of mayors, planners and space designers. "When art and government are equal, it gives people access to beauty. We recently purchased a factory building on the south side which we'll be occupying and developing. After that we hope to purchase some empty homes and get some new bus lines running through the community."

"Amazing activism," I said.

"Oh, we're not activists," Laker said. "We don't want to be seen as being on one side or another. We just want to improve our quality of life. We want to make people happy. It says that in our strategic plan. We want to instigate fun, beauty, and conversation."

That statement helped illuminate the definition of activism for me. For many people, an activist is seen as someone who is strongly against or for something and who speaks out publicly about it. The word conjures up public demonstrations, polarization, signs, loudspeakers. We often see images of activists on both sides of an issue confronting each other in public places. As a journalist, I have photographed many events where people were face to face, shouting at each other about who was right and who was wrong. Dualism at its worst. But dualism is our default mode, given the times and the culture we live in. What's evolutionary, what's truly creative and original, is developing the skills to go beyond duality.

When Baudelaire said that "true genius is the ability to hold two contradictory thoughts simultaneously without losing your mind" this is probably what he had in mind. Practicing this is a prelude to higher consciousness. When we accomplish it—train our minds to make a case for both sides of an argument— it literally changes the architecture of our brain. What we're doing when we unite the opposites is rewiring our brains, creating new neural networks, new pathways that will re-route us from knee-jerk reactions to heart-based responses.

The practice of uniting the opposites means opening the heart as much as the mind. It means feeling our way forward even as we're thinking our way forward, for it is our feelings that rise up like red lights, alerting us to the crossroads of old habits and new choices. There is a momentary discomfort as we try to find the rightness in another's thinking or perceive the "enemy" as our self. It goes against everything we've ever learned, and it leads to the same kind of emotional withdrawal pains that come with every attempt to give up an addiction.

We are addicted to dualism because every institution of our lives has promoted this kind of thinking, but none of us can call ourselves free until we have rid ourselves of this dangerous habit. The ability to hold two contradictory thoughts simultaneously is not just a matter of true genius; it is a matter of true freedom. If we cannot hear an opposing idea without a negative emotional reaction, we are not free. We are bound to a belief that we have most likely inherited and never thoroughly examined.

Creativity is sparked by this kind of radical rethinking. It is a combustion of originality that is rooted in the merging of opposites. Just as a battery is charged by the union of positive and negative forces, just as a child is conceived by the union of a male sperm and female ovum, or a thought issues forth from the union of right and left brain, so does the new emerge—new possibilities, new energy, new directions—when we join "us" and "them" into a "we."

Activism today is outgrowing its duality, taking off its armor, to some extent. Activists today are not necessarily *pro* one thing and *anti* another. Some are engaging in creative endeavors that are for the betterment of all. Some are advocating for the Earth who has no voice to speak out. Some are finding ways to create public conversations that explore the issues that face us as a society.

For one week, I collected clippings of actions by ordinary people that I would classify as activists—people taking public action for the common good. Here are a few examples:

David de Rothschild created a 60-foot sailboat, called the Plastiki, from more than 12,000 recycled plastic bottles and sailed it from San Francisco to Sydney, Australia. The journey was 8000 miles and took 130 days. According to a National Geographic post about the project, "the team aims to captivate and inspire, as well as to motivate tomorrow's environmental thinkers and doers to take positive action for the planet and be smart with waste."

An article on high school activism reveals that high school clubs are taking on more activist roles in the San Francisco Bay area. Africause Club students at Sequoia High School are making and selling bead jewelry and donating the revenue to African causes. The Dream Club raises college scholarship money for undocumented immigrant students. The Human Trafficking Club meets weekly to support the end of trafficking and slavery. There is a Random Acts of Kindness Club that collects canned foods, cleans up the beaches, and performs other community services.

Three teachers who wanted to open a new public school decided to tour the U.S. for 35 weeks and learn best practices from America's best teachers. The project is called The Odyssey Initiative. A Kickstarter campaign was created and 462 backers pledged $82,342 to bring the project to life. The teachers are blogging reports of their findings as they travel. At Manhattan Country School in New York, NY, they asked two questions. When are children capable of understanding social justice? When is it developmentally appropriate to actively engage students in helping their community? They found that social justice and global citizenship is a tenet of the educational mission for all students at Manhattan Country School.

According to the staff, the themes of activism and social justice run throughout the K-8 curriculum, and students engage in the concepts from a young age because they can understand them. In one class of 6-7 year olds, students participate in the Penny Harvest program, a national drive to collect change throughout their school building and turn the change into grants and service projects to better their community.

For retired seniors, the Community Advocacy Network of the Alliance for Retired Americans bridges the missions of the union-based Alliance to community-based organizations. The Alliance for Retired Americans works toward social and economic justice for all citizens. The Community Advocacy Network is a driving force to enroll and mobilize senior and community activists into a nationwide grassroots movement that respects work and strengthens families.

Jane Goodall's *Roots and Shoots* Initiative for Youth offers a myriad of interesting ways for young people of all ages to make the world a better place for people, animals and nature. The Seeds of Peace Program for young leaders has been creating groundbreaking programs around the world for 22 years. There are 5600 alumni continuing to make a difference and a monthly publication, *The Olive Branch,* which is a means for Seeds alumni to sustain communication and share experiences with each other and their communities throughout the school year. For anyone who wants to support the work of these young international peacemakers, they suggest various ways you can help out, from shopping to volunteering, to becoming a Seed or applying to be a counselor at their International Camp. You can also donate to support their programs, learn about hosting a Seeds of Peace event, or apply to join their team of staff and interns.

The Southern Poverty Law Center maintains a *Teaching Tolerance* site that offers a how-to guide for starting a club to address race or gender issues. And another site, The Young America's Foundation, offers tips for organizing for more conservative causes. The Sierra Club has a Facebook page and a Sierra Student Coalition where students can engage in conversations about environmental issues with adults.

If anyone has a burning desire to make a difference or be of use, five minutes with Google will yield plenty of opportunities. When anyone approaches me with the problem, "I'd like to help, but I just don't know what to do," I suggest they bring together the thing they love to do with the thing that's breaking their heart. If you're worried about the oceans, or the rainforest, do a little research. Check out some organizations like Sierra Club, Pachamama Alliance, Worldwatch Institute. See what they're doing, and see if that goes together in any way with something you love doing, like travel, or singing, or golf. Bring together a group of people and brainstorm some ideas. Throw a dinner party with a purpose. The whole point is to have fun, to enjoy others in the process, and to create results that are greater than what you could create by yourself.

Jimmy Schneidewind, a public policy associate at AIDS United, posted an online article comparing the new "soft activism" to "hard activism" which traditionally involves "direct action, boots on the ground, specific goals, and participation that is lower in numbers but perhaps more fervent than that of soft activism." He does a good job of comparing the Baby Boomers' approach to activism with the Millennials' approach and suggesting there is a need for both of them. The modern version of "soft" activism will never replace the old, yet its reach may go further with less energy than the marches and rallies of old. There is a place for wristbands, blogging campaigns, Facebook posts for a cause, online petitions, tweets, likes, and marathons.

Where activists of the sixties and seventies were out to raise a ruckus, today's activists are out to raise awareness, and they do that successfully without leaving home. There is no one way or the other anymore. Remember, true genius comes from holding two opposite thoughts at the same time. Soft activism is great. Hard activism is great.

When Henri Bergson wrote that a "new system of philosophy will only be built up by the collective and progressive effort of many thinkers... completing, correcting and improving one another," he was reminding us that the answers to our most burning questions are already within us and will surface in the context of our sincere conversations with each other. Creating conversations of consequence is one of our greatest challenges.

Modern day Salons are playing an important role in disseminating information, heightening group consciousness, and forwarding action in a variety of arenas. The term Salon was an Italian invention that cropped up early in the 16th century, then spread to France and other countries. Important topics of the day were discussed and Salons, which got their name from the large room in estates in which they were held, led to what became known as "the age of conversation."

As Gertrude Stein was holding Salons in the 1940s in Europe, Perle Mesta became famous in the United States for doing the same. In Washington, DC she was known as the "Hostess with the Mostest" for bringing together Washington's political elite, congressmen, intellectuals, artists and entertainers in her bipartisan soirees. For Perle Mesta, who was active in the National Woman's Party and an early supporter of the Equal Rights Amendment, raising consciousness went hand in hand with raising champagne glasses. Creating Salons was her form of activism and for that she made the cover of *Time* magazine.

In a similar fashion, Ruth uses Salons for her activist work in San Diego. These are her words:

I convene diverse thought leaders in my home to connect, entertain and inspire initiatives for health, well-being and disease prevention. In one month, I held three separate Salons hosting from 45 to 80 people. I usually have a notable leader give a short informational presentation. The invitees are people who can benefit from what that thought leader has to offer, create collaborations, and carry the message out into the community.

But for all that to happen as planned, I have to set the stage by making everyone who steps through my door feel, not only welcome, but an integral part of the Salon. It wouldn't be the same without them and what they bring in terms of content, expertise and collaboratory acumen. Then I make sure that every person there is introduced to every other person, and I start conversation in small groups where there is common interest.

As the conversations grow and people bond, I then provide the best possible gluten free, dairy free and organic food because folks who break bread together create a bond, breaking down barriers that may impede the success of the Salon. After so many years of this type of strategic and purposeful entertaining, I can look back and know that many important connections developed, many issues became more visible, and collaborations I could never have dreamed would occur took flight and have become important initiatives.

At one Salon, we had about 40 people for a day of brainstorming and connecting around the issue of Alzheimer caregiver burnout. Most of the money raised goes for research hunting for a cure for the disease, and few solutions exist for the huge number of caregivers whose lives are spent giving care to its victims. Often, after the patient passes, the lives of the caregivers are so compromised that they fall ill themselves from exhaustion and compromised immune systems.

My idea was to bring people together to discuss caregiver burnout and see if we could come up with some programs for the Alzheimer's Association in our area to address these issues. A year and half later, here are some results of that Salon:

There is a "Wellness Series" that promotes self-care and stress reduction by introducing families to various alternative therapies. Dignity Therapy is being offered for the first time to individuals with dementia. The Water Conservation Gardens at Cuyamaca College is developing new programs for both early and middle stage Alzheimer's. The Alzheimer's Association is partnering with social service organizations in our area to co-create programs for whole families. One new development is the "Family Program," which offers a 3-part series to support children as they cope with a family member who has dementia.

I believe there is great power in gathering together thought leaders and caring citizens to stimulate creative thinking and conjure up a future that respects the needs of a changing population.

While Ruth's Salons focus on health and well-being, another resource for people interested in meeting with others for stimulating conversations in general is *The Sun Magazine*. They have a map of the United States on their website (www.thesunmagazine.org) listing all the Salons in the country where Sun readers are converging. Several local libraries sponsor Salons and a Google search of Conversation Salons will keep you busy for hours.

The World Café (www.theworldcafe.com), originated by Juanita Brown and David Isaacs, enhances the capacity for collaborative thinking about critical issues by linking small-group and large-group conversations. Brown and Isaacs believe that the future is born in webs of human conversation, and that compelling questions encourage collective learning. It is their belief that collectively we have all the wisdom we need, and this wisdom is best surfaced in public conversations.

I had the opportunity to participate in a World Café conversation at a recent conference and the results were fascinating. There were about fifteen tables set up in the room with four chairs at each table. We all took our seats and the facilitator announced that we would have fifteen minutes of conversation on the subject, then three of the four participants would go to other tables, leaving behind one "host" at each table to welcome the three new individuals. The question he posed to the group was "What have you learned in your life about compassion?"

Given the time limitation and the fact that none of us could talk more than four minutes each if we were going to give everyone a chance to talk, we had to get right down to business. Despite the fact that we were four complete strangers, we struck up an immediate intimacy, each of us speaking personally about events in our lives when compassion was called into play. While none of us were attempting to dissect or define the word, the essence of compassion was being articulated through everyone's heartfelt stories. Some confessed to a lack of compassion; some to times when they felt it had been denied them; another, to an experience of how someone's compassion for him enabled him to see a part of himself he had never seen before.

What I noticed most was a complete and sincere engagement of the group in each person's story. The more we leaned in to listen to each person, the more it seemed we were listening each other into being. By the time our fifteen minutes were up, I felt that I had been changed by those brief anecdotes, that somehow compassion had shifted from a concept to a reality that was present, not just at our table, but in the whole room. There was a gentleness in the air.

The facilitator advised three from each table to go to different tables and attempt to deepen the conversation. "Try and take what you have experienced to the next level, " he said. We would have another fifteen minutes. So people brought the most relevant unfoldings from the first conversation to the next, and a deepening, in fact, occurred. At the second table, the conversation shifted from personal to practical. From the personal stories, everyone had come to a new awareness about the power of compassion, and our attention now was on manifesting it more consciously in our lives—actually using it as a force for good or a new approach to conflict. These conversations had a more communal feel to them, as if we were exploring, expanding as a group.

When our time was up, the facilitator engaged us in a large group discussion, so we heard from participants what had happened to them, how they felt about the process, what new insights they'd gained, and the responses were profound. For many people, this was the first time in their lives they had had a meaningful conversation about something that mattered. They were astonished that they could do it with strangers, that they felt safe, that they could learn so much in such a short time from someone else's story. One man had tears in his eyes as he reported to the group, "I've kept myself hidden for fifty years and the big question I have now is 'For what?' What was I afraid of?' I've just learned more in the last half hour than in the last few years of my life."

Dr. Benet Davetian, sociologist, writer, and founder of the Charlottetown Conversation Salon on Prince Edward Island, Canada, writes in his essay, "The History and Meaning of Salons:"

It is in such environments that great ideas are born...and where people find the energy to have a positive influence on the world. The Salon gathering not only satisfies our need for collective effervescence, but also our need to live our individual lives with the certainty that we are visible to others and supported by them.

It does not take millions of people to change social reality. Salons of previous eras have shown that it takes only a handful

of creative and concerned individuals to trigger large scale positive change...The contemporary Salon offers similar opportunities. It facilitates our desire to heal the rifts that have been the
unintended consequences of an overly-rationalized, bottom-line
culture. Conversation Salons are perhaps the new venues for a
new cultural revolution: the revolution of rebuilding and revital-
izing communities and their creative energies. If the numbers
of recently-formed Salons, local discussion groups, and internet
virtual Salons are any indication, we may be witnessing a seminal event in contemporary history: the revival of the ability to
talk with others and relate with them for the simple pleasure of
doing so. And also for the pleasure of contributing to human
progress.[5]

Groups of people are coming together across the country and organizing Salons, databanks, resource materials, curricula for teachers, and
networks for citizens who want to become more active in shaping the
culture that will be our legacy. A brilliant demonstration of collective
genius is underway, providing unlimited portals for participation and
platforms for leaders and cultural creatives who can articulate a vision
for America that works for the children, for the poor, for the earth, and
for business.

In a sense, we are all creators and activists whether we acknowledge
it or not. We create stories all day long. Something happens and we
make up a story about it to tell to our friends. We create everything:
the narrative arc, the hero, the villains, the conflict, the resolution. We
don't think of ourself as a creator, but all day we're creating our life and
coloring it in with our stories, our choices, our prayers or fears.

And somewhere deep in our stories is a hope, a vision, that it will
matter to someone. We are advocating for something, acting in a certain way so that something will occur—and though it may not be for the
rainforests or global warming or to protect the whales or polar bears—
our actions *do* cause change. Our stories *could* be a lifeline for someone

in the dark. They have an impact, for the good or the not-so-good. Metaphorically speaking, our stories will either feel like we're pouring a bucket of ashes or a bucket of rose petals over the person who's listening. They have an energy of their own.

Being mindful of the power of our creations is evolutionary. Just as we have been changed by the creations of others, so are others be changed by ours. And while we cannot *see* the impact of our energy, science provides evidence of our absolute interconnectedness. We all have an electromagnetic energy field that extends eight to ten feet beyond our bodies. Our hearts and brains send out waves that actually register in the bodies of others. A study at the Institute of Heart Math found that that the EKG of one person's heart could be measured in the EEG of another person's brain. This is how intimately we're connected. This is what our oneness is about.

Researchers at HeartMath have measured an exchange of heart energy between individuals up to 5 feet apart. They have found that one person's brain waves can synchronize to another person's heart, suggesting that individuals in a "psychophysiologically coherent state become more aware of the information encoded in the heart fields of those around them." According to the scientists:

> The results of these experiments have led us to infer that the nervous system acts as an "antenna," which is tuned to and responds to the electromagnetic fields produced by the hearts of other individuals. We believe this capacity for exchange of energetic information is an innate ability that heightens awareness and mediates important aspects of true empathy and sensitivity to others. Furthermore, we have observed that this energetic communication ability can be intentionally enhanced, producing a much deeper level of nonverbal communication, understanding, and connection between people. There is also intriguing evidence that heart field interactions can occur between people and animals. In short, energetic communication via the heart

field facilitates development of an expanded consciousness in relation to our social world.[6]

The researchers conclude that heart coherence and social coherence mutually reinforce each other, so that if more individuals consciously increase their positive emotions, psychosocial attunement may also be increased, leading to more coherent and compassionate social relations. An expanded and deepened awareness results not only among and within individuals but in the whole of society.

The visionary leaders and co-creators of this age are speaking out about social interdependence, mindfulness practices, planetary awareness. They are using every network available to evoke spirit, provoke thought, inspire action. Today's activism is as much about consciousness as it is about culture-making. It aims for unity while it expands diversity. Instead of resisting the old, they are creating the new. As Buckminster Fuller said. "To change something, build a new model that makes the existing model obsolete."

Healing the wounds of the earth and its people is an act that, in itself, heals us. It is holy work. It takes the whole body, the whole mind, the whole being, and a feeling for the whole human and planetary organism of which we are a tiny part. As we grow into an awareness of our oneness with creation, so are we discovering our role as makers of history.

A hundred years from now, some descendent of yours may be looking you up to see what actions you took, what issues you spoke out for, what use you made of the time you were given. We all leave our trails, a record of what we did or failed to do. What we create is alive. Our stories, our words, our works—they have an energy, a life of their own. They are woven into the culture like yarn into an afghan. The billions of us here are creating day in and day out. We are creating our lives, our families and communities, our culture and our civilization. Its terrors are ours. Its triumphs are ours. Let us not forget: our bodies are here for a moment, but our imprint is infinite.

END NOTES

CHAPTER ONE

1. Tanya Lewis, "The Roots of Creativity Found in the Brain," *livescience*, September 16, 2013, accessed July 19, 2015, http://www.livescience. com/39671-roots-of-creativity-found-in-brain.html.

2. Alasdair Wilkins, "Our Brains Are Hardwired to Fear Creativity," io9, September 5, 2011. Accessed July 14, 2015. http://io9.com/5837333/ our-brains-are-hardwired-to-fear-creativity.

3. Tom Jacobs, "How Learning Artistic Skills Alters the Brain," *Pacific Standard*, February 11, 2015, accessed July 19, 2015, http://www.psmag. com/health-and-behavior/how-learning-artistic-skills-alters-the-brain.

4. Carl Sagan, *The Cosmic Connection: An Extraterrestrial Perspective.*, Produced by Jerome Agel, (Anchor Press/Doubleday, Garden City, New York. 1973) 189-190.

5. David Lamoureux, "Advertising: How Many Marketing Messages Do We See in a Day?" Fluid Drive Media. Accessed July 14, 2015. http:// www.fluiddrivemedia.com/advertising/marketing-messages/

6. Patrick J. Zirnheld et al. "Haloperidol Impairs Learning and Error-related Negativity in Humans," *Journal of Cognitive Neuroscience*, Vol. 16, No. 6 (2004): 1098-1112. Accessed July 14, 2015. doi:10.1162/0898929041502779.

7. Ruth Westreich and Jan Phillips, "Creativity Survey" (unpublished study, March 7, 2014).

8. Rupal Parekh. "Global Study: 75% of People Think They're Not Living Up to Creative Potential." *Advertising Age*, April 23, 2012. Accessed July 14, 2015. http://adage.com/article/news/ study-75-living-creative-potential/234302/

9. Westreich and Phillips, Creativity Study, 2014.

10. Rollo May, *Courage to Create* (New York: W.W.Norton,1994) 71.

11. Elaine Pagels, *The Gnostic Gospels* (New York: Vintage Books 1979) xiii.

12. Henry Miller, *On Writing* (New York: New Directions: 1957) 25.

13. Tania Lombrozo, "The Truth about the Left Brain/Right Brain Relationship," NPR 13.7 Cosmos & Culture, December 2, 2013. Accessed on July 15, 2015, http://www.npr.org/secti ons/13.7/2013/12/02/248089436/the-truth-about-the-left-brain-right-brain-relationship; Steven Novella, "Left Brain – Right Brain Myth," *Science-Based Medicine*, August 6, 2014. Accessed July 15, 2015. https://www.sciencebasedmedicine.org/left-brain-right-brain-myth/

14. Ruth Westreich, "Divergent and Convergent Thinking in Tandem," July 14, 2015.

15. Amanda Gardner, "Power Naps May Boost Brain Activity," CNN. com25, 2013. Accessed July 15, 2015. http://www.cnn.com/ 2012/10/17/health/health-naps-brain/

16. Jonah Lehrer, *Imagine: How Creativity Works* (New York: Houghton Mifflin Harcourt, 2012)

17. Ibid., xvii.

18. Kabir, *Kabir: Ecstatic Poems,* trans. Robert Bly (Boston: Beacon Press, 2007)

19. Joachin Funke Milieus of Creativity: An Interdisciplinary Approach to Spatiality of Creativity (Knowledge and Space), ed. Peter Meusburger, Joachim Funke, Edgar Wunder (Germany: Springer Science + Business Media B.V., 2009) 15.

20. Diary," Pacific Studio for Dance, accessed July 19, 2015, http://www. pacificstudiodance.com/diary

21. Nancy Andreasen, "Secrets of the Creative Brain," Aspen Ideas Festival, 2014, accessed July 15, 2015, http://www.aspenideas.org/ session/secrets-creative-brain.

22. Alan Hall, "100 Founders Share Their Top 'Aha' Moments – Guess How Many Jobs They've Created So Far?" *Forbes,* October 15, 2012, accessed July 15, 2015, (http://www.forbes.com/ sites/alanhall/2012/10/15/100-founders-share-their-top-aha-moments-guess-how-many-jobs-theyve-created-so-far/)

23. Tim Kreider, "The 'Busy' Trap." *New York Times,* June 30, 2012, accessed July 15, 2015, http://opinionator.blogs.nytimes.com/2012/06/30/ the-busy-trap/?_php=true&_type=blogs&_r=0

24. Duco A. Schreuder, *Vision and Visual Perception: The Conscious Base of Seeing* (Richmond, Canada: Archway Publishing, 2014) 511.

25. New Thought Library: Change Your Life: Books," New Thought Library, accessed July 19, 2015, http://www.newthoughtlibrary.com/holmesErnest/scienceOfMind/som_293.htm

26. Pierre Teilhard de Chardin, *The Phenomenon of Man* (New York: Harper & Row, London: William, 1959) 180.

27. The University of Louisville Photographic Archives houses more than a hundred Dorothea Lange photographs, which were commissioned by the Farm Security Administration and are part of the Roy E. Stryker Collection. These include numerous images captured between May 1935 and February 1939, the period in which Steinbeck researched and wrote *Of Mice and Men and The Grapes of Wrath.*" *University of Louisville University Libraries Research Guides.* Accessed July 15, 2015. http://louisville.libguides.com/lange.

28. "About This Program," National Film Preservation Board, Library of Congress, accessed July 19, 2015, http://www.loc.gov/programs/national-film-preservation-board/about-this-program.

CHAPTER TWO

1. [1] www.thresholdchoir.org

2. USA Today, March 8, 2016. p.4A

3. Malcolm, Ellen, "How Women Crashed the Senate: Emily's List," USA Today, March 8, 2016, p.7A

4. Coleman Barks, *Essential Rumi.* (San Francisco: Harper SF, 1995), 112.

5. http://www.onbeing.org/blog/einstein-sleuthing/3637

6. Ervin Lazslo, *Science and the Akashic Field.* (Rochester, VT: Inner Traditions, 2004), 104.

7. http://sparcinla.org/

8. http://www.huffingtonpost.com/julia-wasson/learning-los-angeles-judy_b_5456151.html

9. http://www.huffingtonpost.com/julia-wasson/post_8090_b_5619289.html

10. Phone interview, February 10, 2014
11. http://www.bigcar.org/events/
12. Kennedy, Randy. (2013, March 20) *"Outside the Citadel, Art That Nurtures"*. The New York Times. Art & Design. p. AR1.
13. http://www.socialpracticesartnetwork.com/
14. http://creativetime.org/

CHAPTER THREE

1. h t t p : / / w w w . s c i e n t i f i c a m e r i c a n . c o m / a r t i c l e / meditation -on-demand/
2. http://www.newbrainnewworld.com/?Science_of_Awakening
3. Andrew Newberg, M.D. and Eugene D'Aquili, M.D., PhD, *Why God Won't Go Away, Brain Science and the Biology of Belief,* Ballantine Publishing Group, 2001. pages 100-107.
4. https://www.sciencedaily.com/releases/2014/10/141028082355.htm
5. Ivanowski, B. and Malhi, G. S. (2007), 'The psychological and neuro-physiological concomitants of mindfulness forms of medita- tion', *Acta Neuropsychiatrica,* 19, pp. 76–91; Shapiro, S. L., Oman, D., Thoresen, C. E., Plante, T. G. and Flinders, T. (2008), 'Cultivating mindfulness: effects on well-being', *Journal of Clinical Psychology,* 64(7), pp. 840–62; Shapiro, S. L., Schwartz, G. E. and Bonner, G. (1998), 'Effects of mindfulness-based stress reduction on medical and pre-medical students', *Journal of Behavioral Medicine,* 21, pp. 581–99.
6. http://www.mindfullivingprograms.com/whatMBSR.php
7. Mark Doty, *Still Life with Oysters and Lemon* (Boston: Beacon Press, 2001) 50.
8. Clarissa Pinkola Estes, *Women Who Run With the Wolves* (NY: Random House, 1992)
9. Anna Wise. The High Performance Mind. (NY: Jeremy Tarcher/ Putnam, 1995).
10. ibid, 2.
11. Journal of Clinical Psychology: In Session, Vol. 69 (8), 1-12 (2013), 2013 Wiley Periodicals, Inc.

12. http://www.newbrainnewworld.com/?Science_of_Consciousness:Interview_with_Erik

13. http://centerformsc.org/self-compassion_test

CHAPTER FOUR

1. http://www.youtube.com/watch?v=3EaUb4zk0Ow

2. www.youthactivismproject.org

3. http://college.usatoday.com/2014/08/18/generation-ideal-millennials-and-social-media-activism/

4. Robert Grudin. *The Grace of Great Things*. (NY: Houghton Mifflin) 1990.

5. http://www.nobelprize.org/nobel_prizes/literature/laureates/1995/heaney-lecture.html

6. http://delong.typepad.com/sdj/2013/09/from-anna-akhmatova-requiem.html

CHAPTER FIVE

1. "Life at IDEO," IDEO, accessed July 16, 2015, http://www.ideo.com/life-at-ideo/.

2. Ibid.

3. David Kelley, "Stop Talking and Start Making," IDEO.com, last accessed July 15, 2015, http://www.ideo.com/people/david-kelley.

4. About IDEO,"IDEO, accessed July 16, 2015, http://www.ideo.com/about/.

5. Ibid.

6. Max Chafkin, "The Ugly Truth about Silicon Valley's Diversity Problem," *Fast Company*, June 2014, accessed July 21, 2015, http://www.fastcompany.com/3029444/the-ugly-truth-about-silicon-valleys-diversity-problem.

7. Financial Tools for Youth," IDEO, accessed July 15, 2015, http://www.ideo.org/stories/kicking-off-with-moneythink.

8. The Huffington Post, "Whole Foods Co-CEO: Executive Pay Caps A Part of Our 'Culture' (Video)," June 18, 2013, accessed July 21,

2015, http://www.huffingtonpost.com/2013/06/18/walter-robb-salary_n_3459029.html

9. Peter M. Senge, *The Fifth Discipline. The Art and Practice of the Learning Organization* (London: Random House, 1990) 3.

10. Elizabeth Debold, "The Business of Saving the World," *What Is Enlightenment?* March-May, 2005, 83.

11. James Surowiecki, *The Wisdom of Crowds* (New York: Anchor Books, 2005) 276.

12. Home," Diversity Connect, accessed July 21, 2015, http://www.diversityconnect.net/.

13. http://www.fastcompany.com/3029444/the-ugly-truth-about-silicon-valleys-diversity-problem

14. Ibid.

15. Max Depree, *Leadership Is an Art* (New York: Bantam Doubleday Dell, 1989) 12.

16. Glenn Hasek, "Millenials Seek Out Companies that Care about the Environment," *Green Lodging* News, February 8, 2008. Accessed July 15, 2015, http://www.greenlodgingnews.com/Millennials-Seek-Out-Companies-That-Care-About-Environment-.

17. Ibid.

18. E.M. Rogers, *Diffusion of Innovations,* 4th ed., (New York: The Free Press, 1995).

19. Melissa Peirce, telephone interview with author, March 5, 2015.

20. Steven Tepper, "Is an MFA the New MBA?" *Fast Company,* March 28, 2013, accessed July 15, 2015, http://www.fastcompany.com/3007541/mfa-new-mba.

21. *David Whyte, Crossing the Unknown Sea: Work as a Pilgrimage of Identity. (New York, Riverhead Books, 2002), 241- 242.*

22. David Whyte, "The Lightest Touch," *Everything is Waiting for You,* Langley, Washington: Many Rivers Press, 2003). (reprinted with permission)

23. Brené Brown, *The Gifts of Imperfection: Let Go of Who You Think You're Supposed to Be and Embrace Who You Are,* (New York: Hazelden Publications, 2010).

24. PricewaterhouseCoopers, *Millenials at Work: Reshaping the Workplace,* 2011. Accessed July 15, 2015, http://www.pwc.com/en_M1/m1/services/consulting/documents/millennials-at-work.pdf.

25. Josh Jones, "Share the Wealth, or Share the Poverty," Guernica, July 5, 2006, accessed July 22, 2015, https://www.guernicamag.com/interviews/either_share_the_wealth/

26. Howard Bloom, *Global Brain: The Evolution of Mass Mind* (New York: John Wiley and Sons, 2000).

27. Viktor Frankl, *Man's Search for Meaning* (New York: Buccaneer Books, 1992) 85.

CHAPTER SIX

1. Susan Froemke, Matthew Heineman, dir., *Escape Fire: The Fight to Rescue American Healthcare,* released October 5, 2012 (Los Angeles, CA: Roadside Attractions, 2012).

2. National Initiative for Arts and Health in the Military, "Arts, Health and Well-being across the Military Continuum: White Paper and Framing a National Plan for Action," accessed July 15, 2015. http://www.americansforthearts.org/sites/default/files/pdf/2013/by_program/legislation_and_policy/art_and_military/ArtsHealthwellbeingWhitePaper.pdf

3. ibid., 17.

4. Gail Rule Hoffman, telephone interview with author, April 2, 2015.

5. Robert Redford, National Arts Policy Roundtable, hosted by Americans for the Arts and the Sundance Institute, October 15, 2013.

6. Sheila Bender. Writing the Personal Essay, (*Writers Digest Books,* 1st Ed., April 1995)

7. John Ruskin, introduction to **Eudora Welty: Photographs** (Jackson: University Press of Mississippi, 1989).

8. Fine Arts Center, Colorado Springs, "In Georgia O'Keeffe's Own Words," accessed July 22, 2015, http://www.csfineartscenter.org/wp-content/uploads/2015/04/OKeeffe-quotes.pdf.

9. Anne Lamott. *Bird by Bird* (New York: Random House, 1994).

10. Westreich, 2014.

11. Ping Ho, e-mail message to author, September 12, 2014.

12. ibid

13. ibid

14. ibid

15. ibid

16. Rachel Naomi Remen, MD, "Healing Yourself," RachelRemen.com, accessed July 21, 2015, http://www.rachelremen.com/learn/self-care/

17. Ibid.

18. The American Art Therapy Association has a research committee which produces a registry of outcome-based research from all the art-therapy disciplines and is available on their website. For more information go to http://www.arttherapy.org/aata-resources.html.

19. Our Mission and Vision," Music & Memory, accessed July 21, 2015, http://musicandmemory.org/about/mission-and-vision/

20. Donna Sapolin, "Bringing Someone with Dementia Back to Life," *nextavenue*, February 18, 2014, accessed July 21, 2015, http://www.nextavenue.org/bringing-someone-dementia-back-life/.

21. Oliver Sachs, *Musicophelia: Tales of Music and the Brain* (New York: Vintage, 2008) 329.

22. Justin S. Feinstein et al. "Sustained Experience of Emotion After Loss of Memory in Patients with Amnesia," *Proceedings of the National Academy of Sciences*, 2010; 107(17), 7674-7679.

23. Barbara Reuer, PhD, e-mail message to author, September 17, 2014.

24. Jim Morelli, MPH, "Movement Helps Movement, Mood in Parkinson's Patients," WebMD, June 20, 2000, accessed July 21, 2015, http://www.webmd.com/parkinsons-disease/news/20000620/music-helps-parkinsons-patients.

25. Gina Kolata, "Learning to Listen," *The New York Times*, December 29, 2009, accessed July 22, 2015, http://www.nytimes.com/2010/01/03/education/edlife/03narrative.html?_r=1&emc=eta1.

26. Cindy Crawford et al., "Sensory Art Therapies for the Self-Management and Control of Chronic Pain," *Pain Medicine* 15 (2014): S66-S75.

27. Johanne Hatteland Somme, "Medical Art Therapy: A Useful Supplement to Classical Medicine?" *Advances in Relational Health,* July 2005 (4)2, 2, accessed July 21, 2015, http://www.bibliopsiquis.com/asmr/0402/Medical.pdf

28. Ed Pilkington, "U S Military Struggling to Stop Suicide Among Military," *The Guardian (US Edition).* February 1, 2013, accessed July 16, 2015, http://www.theguardian.com/world/2013/feb/01/us-military-suicide-epidemic-veteran.

29. David and Lisa Peacock, phone interview with author, April 22, 2015.

30. Ibid

31. Ibid.

32. Darden Smith, National Arts Policy Roundtable, hosted by Americans for the Arts and the Sundance Institute, October 15, 2013.

33. Ibid.

34. Arthur Frank, *The Wounded Storyteller: Body, Illness, and Ethics, 2nd ed.* (Chicago: University of Chicago Press, 2013) xi.

35. Lukasz M. Konopka, "Where Art Meets Neuroscience: A New Horizon of Art Therapy," *US National Library of Medicine* (2014). Accessed July 16, 2015, http://www.ncbi.nlm.nih.gov/pmc/articles/PMC3944420/.

36. Ibid.

37. Emily Dickinson, "The Only News I Know," The Literature Network, accessed July 24, 2015, http://www.online-literature.com/dickinson/452/.

CHAPTER SEVEN

1. http://www.meditationplex.com/nondual-awareness/brain-non-dual -meditation/

2. Lillian Smith. *The Journey.* (NY: World Publishing, 1954).

3. Ladinsky, Daniel. *The Gift,* (NY: Penguin Books, 1999). Reprinted with permission from the author.

4. David R. Loy. *The World Is Made of Stories.* MA: Wisdom Publications, 2010), 27.

5. http://www.goodreads.com/quotes/901290-storytelling-you-know-has-a-real-function-the-process-of

6. Phone interview, March 17, 2016.

7. www.npr.org/thisibelieve/guide.html

8. https://storycorps.org/

9. free download at iTunes Store or Google Play

10. David R. Loy. *The World Is Made of Stories.* MA: Wisdom Publications, 2010), 18.

CHAPTER EIGHT

1. Holmes, Ernest and Kinnear, Willis. *Thoughts Are Things.* (Dearfield Beach, Florida: Health Communications, Inc. 1999),15, 56, 75.

2. Roberts, Jane. *The Seth Material.* (New York:Prentice Hall, Inc. 1970) 123.

3. Tiller, William, Ph.D., Dibble, Walter, Jr. Ph.D., Kohane, Michael, Ph.D. *Conscious Acts of Creation.* (Walnut Creek, CA: Pavior Publishing, 2001).

4. ibid. 382.

5. David Loy. *The World Is Made of Stories.* (MA: Wisdom Publications, 2010), 6.

6. http://www.bibliotecapleyades.net/ciencia/ciencia_psycho08.htm; Reference: Goswami, Amit and Richard E. Reed, Maggie Goswami: *The Self-Aware Universe: How Consciousness Creates The Material World.* (NY:Jeremy Tarcher/Putnam Books, 1993).

7. http://www.youtube.com/watch?v=Rv9zAwi1lF8

8. http://timesofindia.indiatimes.com/city/lucknow/Try-meditation-to-change-emotional-DNA-Expert/articleshow/18176202.cms

9. Joseph Chilton, *The Biology of Transcendence* (Rochester: Park Street Press, 2002), 80.

10. Barry Boyce. "Two Sciences of Mind," Shambhala Sun, September, 2005, 39.

11. https://www.heartmath.org/resources/heartmath-tools/quick -coherence-technique-for-adults/

12. http://www.meditationinitiative.org/facilitator-training
13. Rollin McCraty, Ph.D., and Doc Childre *The Appreciative Heart: The Psychophysiology of Positive Emotions and Optimal Functioning* ; http://store.heartmath.org/s.nl/it.A/id.615/.f
14. https://appreciativeinquiry.case.edu/uploads/HeartMath%20article.pdf
15. https://www.heartmath.org/research/research-library/intuition/electrophysiological-evidence-of-intuition-part-1/
16. Rainer Maria Rilke. *Letters to a Young Poet.* (NY: W.W. Norton & Co, 1934).
17. Lynne McTaggart, *The Intention Experiment* (NY: Free Press, 2007), xxiii.Thomas Berry, *The Great Work* (NY: Random House, 1999).
18. http://www.nytimes.com/2015/12/03/t-magazine/art/theaster-gates-mark-bradford-rick-lowe-profile.html?_r=0
19. https://littlelovinghands.com/about-us
20. Henri Bergson. *Creative Evolution.* (NY: Dover Publications, Inc.), 27

CHAPTER NINE

1. Earle J. Coleman. *Creativity and Spirituality,* (Albany, NY: SUNY Press, 1998), xiv.
2. Wassily Kandinsky. *Concerning the Spiritual in Art.* (Toronto, Canada: Dover Publications, 1997), 33.
3. Alex Grey. *The Mission of Art.* (Boston, MA: Shambhala Press, 1998) 18-19.

CHAPTER TEN

1. Paul Hawken, *Blessed Unrest* (NY: Penguin Group, 2007)
2. Joseph Campbell, *Myths to Live By* (NY: Penguin Books, 1972), 266.
3. In-person interview, June 10, 2004.
4. Phone interview, May 1, 2015
5. www.bdavetian.com/Salonhistory.html

6. Rollin McCraty, Ph.D., Raymond Trevor Bradley, Ph.D. and Dana Tomasino, BA "The Heart Has Its Own 'Brain' and Consciousness." http://in5d.com/the-heart-has-its-own-brain-and-consciousness/

JAN PHILLIPS BIO

www.janphillips.com

JAN PHILLIPS IS a writer, photographer and activist who connects the dots between evolutionary creativity, spiritual intelligence and social action. In her keynotes and workshops, she uses music, poetry and images to keep the heart and brain connected. Jan is the author of ten award-winning books which include *There Are Burning Bushes Everywhere, No Ordinary Time, Finding the On-Ramp to Your Spiritual Path, Finding Ourselves on Sacred Ground, The Art of Original Thinking, Divining the Body,* and *Marry Your Muse.* She has taught in over 25 countries and her work has appeared in the *New York Times, Ms., Newsday, People, Christian Science Monitor, New Age Journal, National Catholic Reporter, Sun Magazine,* and *Utne Reader.*

Jan's quest has led her into and out of a religious community, across the U.S. on a Honda motorcycle, and around the world on a one-woman peace pilgrimage. Blending east and west, art and activism, reflection and ritual, Jan's presentations provoke original thinking and evolutionary action. Jan has three CDs of original music, a YouTube channel, and several DVDs to inspire creativity.

Jan is co- founder and director of the Livingkindness Foundation, a grassroots activist organization supporting women in leadership and art in activism. The Livingkindness Foundation, in collaboration with the NGO Hope for the Village Child, built the Livingkindness Centre for Learning in Ikuzeh, Nigeria. It houses twenty solar-powered computers and has apartments for two full time teachers. *www.livingkindness.org*

RUTH WESTREICH BIO

www.thewestreichfoundation.org

THE WESTREICH FOUNDATION generously supports integrative, functional, palliative and natural medicine nationally and locally, as well as supporting creative and expressive arts as part of whole person healing—body, mind and spirit. Her primary capability is as a connector, bridge and strategist within her focused areas of support.

She is or has been a part of such successful collaborations as the Bravewell Collaborative and Rachel's Network. She has successfully supported Academy of Integrative Health and Medicine; Academic Consortium for Integrative Health, Academic Consortium for Integrative Health and Medicine, American Nutrition Association, UCLA Arts and Healing and many more. She supports programs at Cal State San Marcos, including the Institute for Palliative Care, as well as the Consciousness and Healing Institute and Institute of Noetic Sciences.

Ruth was instrumental in the development of the University of San Diego's Institute for Nonprofit Education and Research by establishing masters and doctorial level of degrees, an applied global research center and certificate programs. She works to build strong women leaders with a number of organizations.

Ruth has over thirty-five years experience as a strategic marketer and cause marketer in both the corporate and nonprofit sectors. She is responsible for the creation of the award-winning business book, *The Art of Original Thinking—The Making of a Thought Leader* written by Jan Phillips. Jan and Ruth also published a Silver Nautilus award winning coffee table photography and poetry book in 2013, *Finding Ourselves on Sacred Ground.* They are currently working on Volume Two, *Finding Ourselves on Common Ground.*

Ruth calls herself an accidental activist being called to stand up, and stand for, food safety, sustainable farming methods and vaccine safety around the globe.